The
Jonathan Hale Farm
A Chronicle of the Cuyahoga Valley

JOHN J. HORTON

Publication of this book has been made possible by the

Clara Belle Ritchie Trust Fund

Publication No. 116

The Western Reserve Historical Society

Cleveland, Ohio
1961

© The Western Reserve Historical Society, 1961

Library of Congress Catalogue Card Number 61-16510

Printed in the United States of America By

Sherman and Son, Cleveland, Ohio

Foreword

In these days of speed and change when scientists are looking for other worlds to conquer, it is sometimes refreshing to stop and ponder a bit over another age not too far distant, when life proceeded at a much slower pace. The first part of the last century saw people come from Connecticut and other eastern states to obtain farms for themselves in our Western Reserve, where even then Indians were still living. Such a man was Jonathan Hale, who, after purchasing land in Ohio from a Proprietor of the Connecticut Land Company, came out in 1810 and settled in what is now Bath Township. This farm has remained continuously in the Hale family. Miss Clara Belle Ritchie, a great-granddaughter of Jonathan Hale, wanting to preserve for the delight and instruction of future generations the manor house and the surrounding acres of the original Hale Farm, left the property in her will to the Western Reserve Historical Society with instructions to care for the property and operate it as a museum to show a way of life that is fast ebbing away.

This book is the story of the Hale Farm. It is written by John J. Horton, based on contemporary accounts and particularly on the diary and letters of Jonathan Hale himself, of which The Western Reserve Historical Society is the fortunate possessor through the kindness and thoughtfulness of Mrs. Frank S. Lally (nee Elizabeth Hale), of Daytona Beach, Florida, a great-great-granddaughter of Jonathan Hale.

Herman L. Vail, *President*

Meredith B. Colket, Jr., *Director*

The Western Reserve Historical Society
Cleveland 6, Ohio

TABLE OF CONTENTS

Foreword

I

THE CUYAHOGA COUNTRY

This is the story of Jonathan Hale, a big, resourceful Connecticut man, trained in the skills of farming, who came to the Western Reserve in 1810 to carve from the wilderness a new home for his family. It is also the story of his farm and the fine brick house he built in the Cuyahoga Valley, and of the children and grandchildren who lived there.

Thanks to source material we shall mention often in this book, we can follow the migration, settlement, and daily life of the Hales in far more detail than we can for any other family which came to the Valley. The story of a single family in the varied and changing migration from the Old Connecticut to the New, can hardly be said to be typical. But that of the Hales is a significant and colorful example, and from it we can learn a great deal that applies to all the Reserve, and in particular to the Cuyahoga country.

But the story of the Hales is necessarily part of a far larger one. To be understood it must go back to the river towns of Old Connecticut where the Hales were born, and whose way of living and religious views they brought to the West. It must include the survey of the land they bought and its purchase from a proprietor of the Connecticut Land Company, the history of the rich Cuyahoga country where they chose to settle, and the development of the little farming community which they helped to grow around them.

The story of the Hales in the West begins with the Cuyahoga. It not only brought the family to this part of the Reserve, because of the fertility of its Valley, but it played a critical role in the history of the country west of the mountains. In many parts of the nation the Cuyahoga would be called a creek. It rises in the hills of Geauga County, east of Cleveland and only fifteen miles south of Lake Erie, into which it eventually empties. Surprisingly, it flows southwest to the ridge which forms the watershed between the Gulf of Mexico and the Atlantic Ocean. At Cuyahoga Falls it turns to the west and at the Portage bends to the north, and from here it winds its pleasant way to the Lake. It is known today primarily for the steel, oil, and other industrial plants which line its banks in Cleveland.

The portion of this little river which has given it practically all its historic importance is only about thirty miles long, from the Portage north to Lake Erie. Up and down this part of the Cuyahoga have traveled the cargo and war canoes of most of the tribes between the mountains and the northern plains of the Mississippi Valley, and later the French, English, and American traders, trappers, explorers, and missionaries. It formed a link between the Lakes and the Ohio River, for at the Portage there was a short and easy carry to the Tuscarawas, the Muskingum, and the trading posts of the Ohio Valley.

The Cuyahoga was chosen for two good reasons over the other streams which wander into Lake Erie—the Huron, the Black, the Chagrin, and the Grand. One reason, of course, was the Portage of a mere eight miles, far shorter and less difficult than any other. The second was the fact that the Cuyahoga, until the settlers cut the forests which stored its water, was more easily navigable, flowing gently with no rapids of any importance. We know that it carried far more water than it does today.

There is evidence that the Mound Builders, a mysterious people, lived in the Valley in the years before history. And we have clearer evidence that the Indian tribe of the Eries lived in the country by 1600, some two centuries before the Western Reserve was surveyed. From the little we know about this tribe, the Eries appear to have been an intelligent, resourceful people. They lived in permanent settlements, which were rare among the Indians, in log cabins roofed with bark and surrounded by palisades. For Indians their agriculture was highly developed. In clearings around their settlements they made small mounds, and in each their women planted beans, corn, and pumpkins which matured in sequence during the summer and fall.

The Eries built forts of earth and logs at strategic locations, on high land commanding the river valleys. There was one on the small plateau across the road from the Hale House, overlooking the river, and probably another on a narrow, mesa-like bluff between Hale Run and Furnace Run, near the village of Everett and a mile or so from the Hales.

The fate of the tribe was mysterious but obviously tragic. The more primitive and warlike Iroquois invaded its land from the East, year after year, until a great battle was fought in 1654 in which the Eries were finally crushed. They were either wiped out or moved further west, but no trace remained of them as a tribe. From that time on, the Valley and its countryside, including most of the Western Reserve, were a sort of no-man's land, with only scattered settlements of Ottawas, a western tribe, and a few Mingoes from the East, an impoverished branch of the Senecas. The country became a hunting ground for whatever Indians were passing through, and most of them followed the Cuyahoga. The river and its portage were covered by a sort of truce, and Indians of many tribes used it as a public highway.

During the eighteenth century the Valley became known to the French and English. On a map made by an American geographer and surveyor named Lewis Evans and published in 1755, the "Cayahaga", as it was often spelled at the time, is described as being "muddy" and "pretty gentle", though Evans' information came at second hand. He also shows a settlement of "Tawas", or

Ottawas, on the east bank of the river about where Boston is today, and this remained a site for Indian settlements until after the white men came. Across the river from the Tawas, Evans shows a "French House", or trading post. Farther south, quite likely on land bought by the Hales, there is a Mingo village.

We have another and first-hand report of what the Valley was like around 1758, from the recollections of Colonel James Smith, written some fifty years later. As a young American soldier in a scouting force under General Braddock, he was captured by Indians in Western Pennsylvania a few days before Braddock's defeat, in 1755. After running the gantlet and watching the Indians burn a number of British prisoners on the river bank at Fort DuQuesne, Smith was ceremoniously adopted by the tribe. For about four years, until he escaped in Canada, he wandered across the Ohio and Lake Erie country as an Indian. It was inevitable that he traveled up and down the Cuyahoga, which he also called the "Cayahaga." He knew the river from the Lake south to what he called the "forks", just beyond Old Portage where the Little Cuyahoga, which he called the "West Branch", joins the river from the South.

"This is a very gentle river," he wrote, "and but few riffles or swift running places, from the mouth to the forks. Deer were tolerable plenty, large and fat; but bear and other game scarce. The upland is hilly and principally second and third rate land"—he was wrong in this—"the timber is black-oak, white-oak, hickory, dogwood, etc." He probably knew it from hunting there.

Smith thought better of the lowland country along the river, like the land on which the Hale House stands today. "The bottoms are rich and large," he wrote, "the timber is walnut, locust, mulberry, red haw, black haw," or hawthorne, "wild apple trees, etc. . . . From the forks I went with some hunters to the East Branch of the Muskingum," the Tuscarawas, that is, "where they killed several deer, a number of beavers, and returned heavy laden with skins and meat."

The skins were cached, or "hung" as Smith put it, at the forks, and the Indians buried their birch-bark canoes nearby, setting out by land for the Big Beaver where they spent the winter. They came back in the spring, laden down with more beaver skins. "When we came to the forks, we found the skins we had folded were all safe. Though this was a public place, and the Indians frequently passing and our skins hanging up in view, yet there were none stolen."

"We took up our birch-bark canoes which we had buried and found they were not damaged by the winter; but they not being sufficient to carry all we had, we made a large chestnut bark canoe, as elm was not found at this place," and the birch was a northern tree. "We all embarked and had a very agreeable passage down the Cayahaga and along the south side of Lake Erie . . ." They sold their skins to French traders at Fort Detroit, and it is significant that they made this long trip rather than sell to the hostile English or Colonials, who by then had captured Fort DuQuesne and renamed it Fort Pitt.

This same country was visited some twenty-five years later by a very different sort of traveler, the Moravian missionary John Heckewelder. He was born in England in 1743, the son of a religious exile from Moravia in the Hapsburg Empire. He came to the Moravian settlement at Bethlehem, Pennsylvania, when he was ten years old and grew up to be a missionary, making a number of trips between Bethlehem and the Christian Indian colonies in Ohio like Gnadenhuetten and Schoenbrunn. During the Revolution, in 1781, the British moved the Christian Indians to the Sandusky River as a precautionary measure and Heckewelder was held a prisoner near Detroit. While he was there, a number of his Indians returned to the Tuscarawas where they were senselessly and brutally murdered by the Americans.

After the war, in 1786, Heckewelder founded a tiny missionary post with the lovely German name of Pilgeruh, or Pilgrim's Rest, near Tinker's Creek on the Cuyahoga. After a year in the place, where he came to know the river well, he went back to Bethlehem. From there he made further journeys to Ohio, principally to Gnadenhuetten. Heckewelder knew the Cuyahoga, which he spelled "Cujahaga" in German fashion, and the country around it as well as any white man of his time. In 1796 he published a map of the country along Lake Erie, including the Moravian settlements to the south, and for it he wrote some notes, dealing almost entirely with the "Cujahaga."

Among the rivers of the area, he wrote, "the Cujahaga certainly stands foremost," and he gave his reasons. Small sloops could come into the mouth of the river for a harbor and there were also fisheries there. The river was also "navigable at all times with Canoes to the Falls, a distance of upwards of 60 miles by water—and with Boats at some seasons of the Year." He thought that with a little expense it could be "made Navigable for boats that distance at all times."

He also spoke of the Portage as "the best prospect of Water Communication from Lake Erie into the Ohio, by way of the Cujahaga and Muskingum Rivers," and that the "carrying places be the shorter of all carrying places, which interlock with each other, and at most not above four miles." This was an underestimate, for the usual portage route was eight miles long. He called Old Portage "Cujahaga Town" and thought it a "remarkable situation for a town" because there the portage route crossed the Indian track from Sandusky and Detroit to Pittsburgh. This was in fact a forecast of the prosperity of Akron, though that city has grown for quite different reasons.

Like everyone else who knew it in these early days, Heckewelder praised the bottom lands along the river, and it was these which interested Jonathan Hale. The Cuyahoga had, "I verily believe, as rich bottoms or intervals as in any part of the Western Country," by which he meant Ohio. "The Timber in these are either Black Walnut or White Thorn Trees intermixed with various other Trees as Cherry, Mulberry, etc. The ground entirely covered with high Nettles." In other bottoms, somewhat inferior to the rest, he found a wider variety of trees, "lofty Oaks, Poplars or Tulip Trees," he was the only traveler to mention the tulip, "Elm, Hickory, Sugar Maple . . . Wild hops of an excellent quality grow also plentifully on this River." The trees interested all these early travelers for the reason that not much else on the land was visible beneath the enormous, tangled growth which covered the upland, hillsides, and bottom land, and overhung the banks of the river.

Drawing on his accurate knowledge of the Cuyahoga, Heckewelder goes on: "The richest land on this River lieth from where the road crosseth the old Town, downward"—that is, from Old Portage north to the Lake. "But within 8 or 10 miles of the Lake," about as far up the river as Pilgeruh, "the bottoms are small, yet the land is rich. From here upwards they are larger and richer . . . The Cujahaga Country abounds in Game such as Elk, Deer, Turkeys, Raccoons, etc. In the year 1785 a trader purchased 23 Horseloads of Peltry from the few Indians trading on this River." Heckewelder's mention of elk is unique and possibly an error, but it is interesting to note that the Indians were "few."

Heckewelder added to his notes a map he drew of the Ohio country, dated 1796, the year in which General Moses Cleaveland and his party began the survey of the Western Reserve. He shows Pilgeruh still on the river near Tinker's Creek. And he also shows a road, or path, in addition to the water route up the Cuyahoga. It began at the mouth of the river and crossed Tinker's Creek not far from Pilgeruh, then cut inland toward the future sites of Hudson, Stow, and Tallmadge, where it joined the path from Sandusky through Old Portage and continued on to the Mahoning and the well-known salt springs near Youngstown. It was a sign that travel in canoes or boats along the river route was near an end, until the building of the canal, and that there was need for routes by land for men and horses, and in a few years more, for wagons.

White men did not come to settle in the Valley between Boston and Old Portage until after 1800. They found a scattering of rather shiftless Indians, mostly around Boston. North of the present village and east of the river there was a camp of Ottawas under a chief named Ponta, or Pontey. The site was known as "Pontey's Camp" until about 1812. South of Boston there was another camp, under a Mingo chief named Stigwanish or Seneca. He was friendly with the whites until the War of 1812, when he sided with the British and disappeared from the Valley. The Mingo camp which can still be traced on the Hale property, east of the road and toward the river, had vanished by the time the white men arrived, or perhaps had moved north to Boston. But wandering Indians appeared in the settlements for years, reduced to doing odd chores or begging, and as late as the Census of 1820, eight were listed as living in Hudson.

Tales of the Indians in the Valley lasted on long after redmen disappeared. There is a story that the Mingoes in Stigwanish's camp had a wooden image of what was probably their god of war. Before they set out on a warlike expedition, the legend goes, they held feasts and war dances before this figure, and hung tobacco around its neck. When the warriors had gone, the bolder white men stole the tobacco, which they said was good.

The first white men who came to this rich and attractive country were the traders or an occasional missionary who passed up and down the river between the Portage and the Lake. But by 1800 a few trappers or hunters had made the country their headquarters and some of them lasted on until the settlers came, about ten years later. One of these legendary figures was Jonathan Williams, who hunted up and down Yellow Creek. Another was William Coggswell, whom an early historian describes as "one of the most expert hunters ever in this part of the country, and there is scarcely a hill or vale that has not echoed to the sharp retort of his rifle." He shot the bear and wolves which menaced the settlers' sheep and hogs, and they traded him pork for venison, which was too dry for a steady diet. He probably had a primitive shack in the forests of Bath or Granger Townships and planted a little corn and beans or pumpkin. For the rest he lived off the woods, the wild grapes and other berries, and the game.

Word of this wild, rich country naturally filtered back east. It brought the first settlers in the years after 1800, squatters who had a love of an adventurous life in the wilderness and a hunger for something new. But they had no legal claim to the land they settled on. Most of them came from the western fringe of settlements in New York and Pennsylvania. Some of them came alone and on foot with packs on their backs; others led horses, and their wives and a child or two walked and rode by turns. But the land in the Valley where the squatters hacked small clearings out of the enormous forests and built their shacks or cabins, already had owners like Jonathan Hale and Jason Hammond, and how they came to possess this land is a complex, intriguing story.

II

THOMAS BULL AND THE WESTERN RESERVE

On a June day in 1810, Jonathan Hale of Glastonbury, Connecticut, bought from Thomas Bull of Hartford five hundred acres of wilderness. In the deed the land was precisely described as lots 11, 12, 13, and part of lot 14 in Township 3, Range 12, of the Connecticut Western Reserve. This dry description was as familiar and full of meaning to many Connecticut people in 1810 as street, number, zone, and city addresses are today.

These forgotten lots, townships, and ranges formed the pattern for the sale and settlement of almost all the land in the Western Reserve. Their outlines have left their mark in county roads and city streets, the boundaries of towns and cities, the shape and size of farms and real estate allotments.

The manner in which Jonathan Hale's five hundred acres were carved from the virgin forest of valley and upland in what today is Bath Township, was the usual procedure for the rest of the Reserve. It was a long, intricate, fascinating process. For the Hale lots it is the story of a land-hungry Connecticut and of the Company whose shareholders gambled on the future of the West, of the woodsmen-surveyors Abraham Tappan and Rial McArthur, of the shrewd land agent Turhand Kirtland, and of Thomas Bull, the stolid Hartford merchant, who never laid eyes on the acres he bought and sold.

The name "Western Reserve" has an odd sound to people who have not grown up with it or lived with it for a while. But it is one of the few regional names in the country which has real meaning. It is not borrowed with a display of classical learning from an English sovereign or proprietor, like Virginia, the Carolinas, or Pennsylvania. Nor is it the distorted French or English version of an Indian word whose meaning is dubious or forgotten, like Massachusetts, Illinois, or Ohio. It means just what it says. It is a sensible, descriptive name like Great Falls or Stony Ridge. There is a matter-of-factness about it which speaks of Connecticut.

The Connecticut Western Reserve was the price the State accepted for yielding its claim to a strip of rich land across the Northwest Territory. The Connecticut claim was old but fantastic. It was based on the Charter King Charles II granted the Colony with a royal flourish in 1662, giving it rights to a strip of land between 42° 2', which ran north of the Reserve in Lake Erie, and 41°, which the surveyors missed by a few miles to the south. For the Reserve, a rough 42°, south to 41°, will do for the layman. The grant ran from the *eastern* border of Pennsylvania to the Western Sea.

When Massachusetts, New York, and Virginia bartered away rather similar claims to land in the Northwest Territory, which vastly increased the prestige of the new Federal Government, Connecticut bargained before it would go along. It was a small state, poor in good farm land, and chronically over-populated. In 1786 Connecticut agreed to abandon the balance of its western claims on the condition that it keep the Western Reserve.

For fifteen years this rich tract, extending 120 miles along the shore of Lake Erie, remained in point-of-law a province of Connecticut, though its scanty population did not require the State to set up a government there. But as the lands were sold and settlers began to drift in, something had to be done. To tie the Reserve to the government in Hartford was clearly impractical, and the people all over Ohio were yearning to become a State. Facing the facts, Connecticut ceded all of its rights in the Western Reserve to the Federal Government, which in turn conveyed back to the State the full ownership of the land itself, without the powers or duties of government. Three years later the Western Reserve became part of the State of Ohio as Trumbull County.

Even before the matter was settled, Connecticut had in effect disposed of the land. As early as 1788 it had sold 25,000 acres known as the Salt Spring Tract to General Samuel Parsons. This was an area near Warren whose deposits of salt were well known to the Indians and the deer. But to sell the balance of the Western Reserve in this way, parcel by parcel, was beyond the capacities of the state government of Connecticut. In 1792 the far western portion, approximately 500,000 acres and known as the Firelands, was set aside for the benefit of the "sufferers" whose towns had been burned by the British during the war. The balance was hopefully estimated at more than 3,000,000 acres and it was sold in 1796 to the Connecticut Land Company for $1,200,000 in promises-to-pay. The State planned to use the money to endow its schools, but it was slow in coming. A survey of the Reserve made many years later by Leonard Case showed that the land actually sold to the Company was around 2,500,000 acres.

Probably no one in Hartford had seen in person the enormous assets of the Company when they were divided on paper into 400 shares, a number which was far too small. There were 35 shareholders in the Company, though at least 49 individuals were involved because some had invested as a group. They were mostly Hartford or Connecticut merchants and speculators in land, and a typical group-investment was one made by James Bull of Hartford, Aaron Olmsted, and John Wyles, and Bull's holdings were apparently sub-scribed in part by his brothers Michael and Thomas. Eventually Thomas acquired all the shares of the family, as we shall see. There was nothing static about the ownership of the land in the Western Reserve.

The amount of land eventually allotted each shareholder depended, of course, on the proportion he owned of the 400 shares, valued at $1,200,000, or $3,000 a share. The result was enormous and decimal confusion, a challenge to IBM. Oliver Phelps, for instance, who invested $168,185, more than anyone else, was legally entitled to 56,061 shares. Sylvanus Griswold, who put in his savings of $1,683, the smallest amount, had .561 of a share. To simplify matters somewhat, the shareholders deeded their holdings in trust to Jonathan Brace, John Caldwell, and John Morgan. They became famous names in the Western Reserve, for it was actually they who signed almost all the deeds issued on behalf of the Company.

*   *   *   *   *   *

Nothing could be done to dispose of this fabulous holding until the land had been surveyed into salable units. The Ohio Land Company, whose lands lay just to the south, had already divided its tract into townships six miles square. As Christopher Sherman, the surveyor of modern Ohio, remarked, "Six-mile townships had been proposed earlier by Connecticut officials but were abandoned . . . perhaps because Congress was considering the use of five-mile townships for its military bounty lands." But at the time, five-mile townships were an innovation.

The survey began in 1796 when Moses Cleaveland, a proprietor, led a party of men to the mouth of the Cuyahoga, the first representatives of the Company to see the land as far as we know. The 177 townships laid out by these courageous men and the others who followed them in the next eleven years, are not precisely five miles square and their number has often changed. For the most part the townships on the level land have only minor deviations, due to primitive instruments, occasional lack of skill, and the stubborn lines of the five-mile survey which ignored the rivers, creeks, and ridges as well as the almost impenetrable forests and swamps. Along the slanting shore of Lake Erie and the meandering lower reaches of the larger rivers, the townships are larger or smaller than the rest as circumstances required, and at the western end adjoining the Firelands there were troubles with the survey of the boundary line which led to somewhat smaller townships in the 19th Range of the Reserve.

But it is wrong to complain. Most of the men were sick at one time or another of the "fever and ague", and many died. In spite of faults, all but 24 of the townships they surveyed do follow the general pattern of five square miles from the Pennsylvania line to the boundary of the Firelands.

Working west from the Pennsylvania line, which was already established, the crews surveyed the townships first, leaving the lots until later. Many of their lines survive today in the regular pattern of county roads. The townships were numbered by ranges from east to west, and by townships within each range from the south to the Lake. Thus the land bought by Jonathan Hale lay in the twelfth range from the Pennsylvania line, and the third township from the southern boundary of the Reserve. This clumsy-seeming numbering system became a part of the everyday speech of the country, and it was used for mailing addresses long after the townships had acquired names.

However, these early surveys stopped at the historic line of the Cuyahoga, the Portage, and the Tuscarawas. For some twenty years in fact this line was a part of the western boundary of the United States. It was first established in the Treaty of Fort McIntosh in 1785, between the United States and the unruly tribes of the Ohio Country—The Delawares, Shawnees, Ottawas, Wyandots, and Potawatomies. But it was not made truly effective until after the Battle of Fallen Timbers ten years later, when General Anthony Wayne imposed on the beaten Indians the Treaty of Greenville. This set up a boundary which followed the old Cuyahoga, Portage, Tuscarawas line to the southern boundary of the present Stark County. From here it slanted southwest to Fort Loramie in Shelby County, then slightly northwest to Indiana. It gave two thirds of Ohio to the white man. But it meant that the land which Jonathan Hale eventually bought from Thomas Bull lay behind the barrier, in what amounted to foreign soil. For a decade the land west of the Cuyahoga remained a sort of no-man's land, hunted occasionally by the Indians, invaded now and then by white hunters and trappers.

*   *   *   *   *   *

Once the eastern township lines were surveyed, the division of the land began. The method used was an old one, common to Connecticut towns for a century or so. In Glastonbury, for instance, the ancestors of Jonathan Hale, being among the original proprietors, drew lots for the common lands of the town on at least two occasions. It was natural to apply this familiar usage to the Western Reserve.

The method used later for all the townships in the Reserve was worked out in the first "draft", or drawing of lots. It was made in 1798 for almost half of the land lying east of the Cuyahoga. The acreage included in the selected townships was divided among the shareholders in proportion to their investment in the Company. It was computed that each township in this initial draft represented $12,903.23 of the total investment of $1,200,000. The shareholders were then arbitrarily grouped into "classes", so that the total share of each class came to the $12,903.23 required for a township. Sometimes a class was composed of one man, often of five or six. The ceremony of drafting, or drawing by lot, was held in the offices of the Company in Hartford.

In all these drafts each class naturally drew one township. The important matter of dividing the land among the members of a class, if there was more than one, was a problem which lasted for years. It plagued the surveyors and ended in amazing confusion. In brief, the proprietors varied in number from township to township and so did their notions about dividing the land. As we have seen, their shares in the Company could be figured to the penny and were almost never the same, and this caused obvious wrangles. As a result, a neat and uniform pattern was usually impossible or ran against the proprietors' interests because of the uneven quality of the land.

To settle the problem in a large majority of the townships, each proprietor in a class received by negotiation or by lot what was known as a tract, a section, or a subdivision which contained his rightful share of the land. He could divide this into lots as he pleased. In some of the townships, especially those in the east, there was no uniform size or shape to these lots, and along the slanting shore of Lake Erie and the banks of the larger rivers the confusion was even worse. In a few towns like Tallmadge elaborate planning was done, for its roads were laid in the design of a six-pointed star centering in the village itself.

But attempts were made in a good many townships to arrive at a more orderly partition, and perhaps the most sensible one was that first suggested by the Land Company itself in April, 1796, two months before General Cleaveland's surveying party set out for the West. It involved four townships, and though the plan was not carried out, it was borrowed in whole or part for a large number of other townships. In the ideal cases discussed in Hartford, the township was surveyed into 100 acres, ten to a side. In Hartford this meant that the lots in the township of 160,000 acres, which was standard, contained 160 acres each. In the practical application of this plan in the field, very few of the townships measured precisely 160,000 acres, nor did all the lots contain 160. To anticipate somewhat, the three full lots which were bought by Jonathan Hale in Township 3, Range 12 varied from 140 acres to 179. These inaccuracies were due of course to the forest and terrain, the lack of experience on the part of some of the surveyors, and the rather primitive instruments they had to use.

In about 12% of the townships in the Reserve this plan was used to survey all the lots, and among them were Bath and Hudson in the Cuyahoga country. There were more in the western townships than those in the east. Northfield is an example of a reason the plan could not be universally used, for although 90% of its upland was surveyed into square 160-acre lots, the balance lay on the wooded sides of the gulls running down to the river and had to be surveyed accordingly. The total lots, however, added up to a hundred. Some of the proprietors in their tracts, sections, and subdivisions laid out such lots, but they formed only parts of the townships.

But there was still another complication—the varying quality of the land made the drafts unfair, for a man might receive only inferior land, such as bog that could not be farmed. To compensate for this, the Company set aside a few "Equalizing Townships" surveyed into strips or tracts. These were attached to the townships where land was poor. Northampton adjoining Bath to the east was one of these equalizing townships and suffered the unhappy effects of absentee ownership.

There was another draft in 1802, which distributed most of the land remaining east of the Cuyahoga, and the value of each township this time came to $13,333,333, a remarkable figure indeed. Though very little of this land east of the Greenville boundary had as yet been sold to settlers or cleared for farming, pressure grew among the shareholders to acquire from the Indians the remaining land to the west. And the "sufferers" in the Connecticut towns and countryside which had been burned by the British clamored for the acres due them in the Firelands still further west.

From what happened it is clear that the Connecticut Land Company and the Firelands Company were largely responsible for the Indian treaty which gave them the rights to this land. They were the principal benefactors and both were represented in the council or "treaty" held with the Indians. Neither the State of Ohio, which had an obvious interest, nor the State of Connecticut were represented at all.

In any event, the Federal Government, prodded no doubt from Connecticut, decided in the spring of 1805 to open negotiations with the Indian tribes to "buy" the land from the Indians, at the usual nominal price. Aside from the desires of the two land companies, there seems to have been no other good reason to force the issue at the time.

The story has been told by Abraham Tappan, in the account of the survey of these western lands which he wrote late in life—or apparently dictated to his daughter. In 1805 Tappan was surveying land in what is now Lake County, then part of Geauga, for General Henry Champion, one of the directors of the Connecticut Land Company, who owned vast acreage in this part of the Reserve. Tappan was either present himself at the proceedings which followed or heard of them from General Champion at first hand. The story he tells is in part a forgotten chapter in the early history of Cleveland, at the time a hamlet of three or four houses on the bluff above the Cuyahoga and of considerably less importance than its neighbor, Newburgh. However it was an excellent site for a council, for it was the point where the east-west trail along the lake met the north-south trail on the Cuyahoga.

"Cleveland," Tappan wrote, "was designated as the place for holding the Treaty," using the word as the Indians did, for the council which produced an agreement rather than the document they were unable to read. Tappan goes on:

> The Indians to the West having claims to the land in question, were invited to attend the council at that place. The Indians residing in Western New York having some claims to the land sent a deputa-

tion of not far from 30 of their members to attend the Treaty at Cleveland. They arrived at the place in June, accompanied by Jasper Parish, their interpreter. The Treaty was held under the auspices of the United States Government. Commissioners from the different parties interested in the Treaty were promptly and in season at the contemplated Treaty ground.

On the part of the General Government, Colonel Jewet was the Commissioner, a very large, muscular man. On the part of the Connecticut Land Company, General Henry Champion appeared as Commissioner. General Champion was also of more than common size and a man of good talents. Roger A. Sherman appeared as Commissioner on the part of the Sufferers, or Fire Land Company.

Sherman was the son of a signer of the Declaration of Independence and the three rather overpowering men were certainly a match for the Indian chiefs. But it is probable that "Colonel Jewet", on behalf of the Government, acted merely to support the claims of the two other commissioners and work out a deal with the Indians. When the "Treaty" finally met, the Indians included the familiar Ohio tribes, the Ottawas, Wyandots, Delawares, Shawnees, and Potawatomies. Tappan goes on:

For some cause the Indians living in the West and interested in the subject matter of the Treaty refused to meet the Commissioners in Council in Cleveland, and but few of them appeared at the place, if we except the deputation from New York. After staying a few days in Cleveland, and being well assured that the Indians would not meet them there, the Commissioners proceeded Westward; and [after] some delay, as show of great reluctance on the part of the Indians, they finally succeeded in meeting them at some place in the vicinity of Maumee Bay. At this Treaty the Indians relinquished their claims to all lands belonging to the Western Reserve west of the Cuyahoga River, as they had done ten years before [at Greenville] to the Company in the East of the River.

This council, so important for the Western Reserve and the settlers who were to cross the Cuyahoga, was held at a little post called Fort Industry on the site of Toledo. Had the Indians been less stubborn, the treaty would have borne the name of Cleveland. The Treaty of Fort Industry served primarily the purpose of the two land companies, for it merely moved the Greenville line to the western boundary of the Reserve, including, of course, the Firelands. It followed the western boundaries of Huron and Erie Counties, continuing south of the Reserve to a point where it met the old Greenville line, south of Mount Gilead. It not only opened the balance of the Reserve and the Firelands to settlement, but quite incidentally, it seems, it also opened the counties of Wayne, Ashland, and Richland, and parts of Holmes, Morrow, and Crawford—some of the richest land in Ohio.

But there was an ominous note at Fort Industry. "It was said by those who attended the Treaty," Tappan wrote, no doubt quoting General Champion, "that as a general thing the Indians in parting with and making sale of the above land to the Whites were not well pleased, and after the Treaty was signed, many of them wept."

The treaty had in fact been extracted from the tribes without more reason than the Connecticut hunger for land. The Indians naturally thought of revenge. The fear of a reprisal hung like a nightmare over the settlers who first crossed the Cuyahoga. The tears of the Indians at Fort Industry were in good part the cause of the uprising under Tecumseh in 1811 and of the Indian war parties which flocked to the aid of the British in the fearful summer of 1812.

*   *   *   *   *   *

With title to the land west of the Cuyahoga now cleared, the Connecticut Land Company could proceed with its surveying. The survey of the important southern boundary of the Reserve, west of the old Greenville line, was done by the Federal Government, presumably because it was also the boundary of public land to the south. In the summer of 1806, Albert Gallatin, Secretary of the Treasury, selected the veteran surveyor Seth Pease to do this job. He had been a member of Moses Cleaveland's party in 1796 as "astronomer and surveyor" and had surveyed in Euclid and Cleveland Townships, among others. In fact he had drawn the second map of the hypothetical City of Cleveland, only a few months after Amos Spafford had drawn the first.

Even before Pease had begun his work, General Champion, as a director of the Connecticut Land Company, had reached an agreement with Abraham Tappan to survey the township lines in the new tract west of the Cuyahoga. Tappan at the time was still working for Champion in Lake County and had recently surveyed the "Village platte of Painesville." It was natural that the General should choose him for the job.

Assisting Tappan were Captain James A. Harper of Harpersfield, who took half of the job, and one Aaron Sessions who probably traveled with Tappan. Following the practice east of the Cuyahoga, they were to survey only the township lines, to prepare for a draft, and the lot lines would come later. Tappan and Harper were to cover 830,000 acres, exclusive of the 500,000 or so in the Firelands which were surveyed by Almon Ruggles.

Tappan's party of fifteen met in Cleveland, which, small as it was, served as headquarters for the work and for many other activities of the Land Company and its agents. Besides the three surveyors there were ax men, with the back-breaking job of hacking a path for the survey, the chain carriers who followed along, pack horses and drivers with supplies and equipment, one half-breed handyman, and a "worthless Englishman" who was fired for drinking.

On May 17, 1808, Captain Harper "with his complement of hands" and pack horses, set out to run the western line of the 11th Range, which of course was also the eastern line of the 12th. It had already been run from the lake to the bank of the Cuyahoga in Northfield Township, and Cleveland, Newburgh, and part of Independence Township lay in the 12th Range east of the river. Harper crossed the river to Brecksville and continued the line south to the southern boundary of the Reserve. It forms the eastern line of Brecksville, Richfield, Bath, Copley, and Norton Townships.

Thus, in Township 3, Range 12, which is now called Bath, Captain Harper and his men surveyed the eastern boundary of lot 11, in which the Jonathan Hale House now stands. Other white men passing this way as traders, explorers, or missionaries had logically followed the river, a few hundred yards farther east in Northampton Township. It is likely, then, that Captain Harper and his men were the first white men to set foot on the lands of Jonathan Hale barring a possible hunter or two. From the summit of the ridge which lies across the road from the house, they could see its site, or the virgin timber which covered it. This was probably in the late afternoon of May 18, 1808.

On the same day, Tappan wrote, "I started with my party of hands to take the traverse of the Portage Path, between the Cuyahoga and the Tuscarawas. . . . I had taken the traverse of the portage path and was proceeding with the traverse of the Tuscarawas southwesterly when Captain Harper and his party finished running the 11th Range and struck the river (the Tuscarawas) with said line but a few minutes before my arrival." This was the 22nd of May.

While Tappan and his men went back to the Cuyahoga end of the portage and began a traverse of the Cuyahoga down to the lake, Harper measured the usual five miles west on the southern boundary of the Reserve to begin the western meridian for Range 12, "and ran said line to the Cuyahoga, striking the river a few miles south of Cleveland." Today this place lies in the flats north of the Clark Avenue Bridge. The hard trip down and back had taken Harper thirteen days. Considering the rugged valley country of most of the line, going south, at least, this was very good time.

The surveyors then began to establish the other meridians, or north-south township lines, all the way west to the 18th. Here all of Tappan's lines came to an end because the Firelands boundary, at the 19th meridian, had not yet been established, and because of an error by Seth Pease on his line for the southern boundary, caused a great deal of trouble. As they worked across country the two parties ran into swamps so deep that the pack horses had to skirt them, and on one occasion the horses and men got lost and the surveyors went without food for a day. In another place the party crossed an area where a tornado had leveled the forest and again the horses were forced to make a circuit around it. In the summer the heat within these great virgin forests was tropical, locked by the vines which laced the top of the oaks and chestnuts and beeches into a dim, green-lit furnace below. In the swamps and wet lands the mosquitoes were almost intolerable, for both men and horses. But of hardships nothing whatever is said in Tappan's chronicle, except the detours of the pack train.

By early July the meridians were finished. Tappan came east to his Cleveland base but set out at once to run the east-west parallels, over the same ground. He began with the second parallel between Bath and Copley. "I began at the Cuyahoga Portage," the only familiar landmark in the area, "and ran west to the 18th Meridian. Whole distance 36 miles. This line almost without exception was over good land." He came back to the river by surveying the first parallel, five miles south.

"July 12th the 3rd parallel or line between the 3rd and 4th Townships was run by Captain Harper and his party." This, of course, was the line between Bath and Richfield, only a lot-width from the Hale lands. "He began on the 12th of July, starting from the West bank of the Cuyahoga," in Everett, that is, a little south of the bridge over the river. Moving west, Harper passed close to the site of the covered bridge over Furnace Run. "He reached the 18th Meridian on July 18th," Tappan reports. "According to his field notes, the quality of the land throughout the whole line is represented as being very good."

Once the parallels were surveyed, the next step was up to the Company. It involved the curious process called "equalizing". During the survey Tappan wrote, "I had been in frequent correspondence with the Agent, Judge Kirtland." This was Turhand Kirtland who lived in Poland in the southeast corner of the Reserve. "I had informed him of the probable time of our finishing the running of the Township lines. It was an Object of the Gentleman," who was the Company's principal representative on the scene, "to assemble the Equalizing Committee at an early period; to make their exploration of the different townships and agree upon the quantity of land to be surveyed into equalizing lots before the season closed. And also to enable the Directors of the Company to make divisions of their land, early in the following winter." It was this same pressure to finish the job and dispose of the lands of the Company which had led to the Treaty of Fort Industry.

"On finishing the running of the Township lines I went to Poland to see the Agent, who accompanied me back to Cleveland. The Agent made his arrangements to have the Equalizing Committee meet at the Cuyahoga Portage the 1st day of September in order to proceed with the explorations." This, of course, was the best time of year for such work in the Western Reserve.

The Equalizing Committee was a distinguished one. Turhand Kirtland himself was a member, and the others were General Martin Smith of Vernon, now called Campbell, and Eliphalet Austin, the proprietor of Austinburg.

"Whilst at Cleveland," Tappan says, "Judge Kirtland in Concurrence with Judge Austin"—judges in the Reserve were as common in those days as colonels in Kentucky—"engaged me to accompany the Committee in this route through the different townships, offering the same pay that the individual members of the Committee received; that was two dollars and fifty cents per day, and all expenses paid," not bad for the times. This was a wise decision on the part of the Committee, for Tappan of course had traversed the region north and south and east and west, and his field notes were helpful too.

Tappan then gives us a brief first-hand glimpse of the neighborhood of the Portage in the early days of its settlement. "At the time set for the Committee to meet," he says, "they assembled at Aaron Norton's in Northampton. Norton lived about two miles easterly from Cuyahoga Portage." In 1803 Norton had built a grist mill on Mud Creek where it crosses Route 8 today, the first mill in this part of the country, and he later added a sawmill as well. In 1810 Jonathan Hale made a trip to these "Northampton mills" a day or so after his arrival in the Valley.

Tappan continues, "At that time no persons lived at the Portage; Norton was the nearest except one family, living a mile down the river," which would put their cabin near Smith Road, "commonly known by the cognomen of 'Old Geer'." With this exception, "at the period I am writing not one person, White, Red, or Black, lived in the tract of country we were to explore. The necessary consequence was, every article of supply had to be carried with us." Thanks to Kirtland, who had the usual contemporary western taste for whiskey, "a little old Monongahela, then a favorite beverage, was snuggly stowed away in the baggage."

The party set out without Judge Austin, and he had little to do with the work of the Committee. The party included Kirtland, General Smith, Tappan and "an Irishman named Wilson, with a packhorse to carry the Provisions and Tent for use of the party." The tent was a most unusual luxury for travel in this part of the world.

The method used by the Equalizing Committee was simple but thorough, considering the problems of terrain and supply. The party left Norton's place and traveled west through the second tier of townships, beginning with Copley, coming back through the first tier along the border. It spent a day in each township and the trip out and back took fifteen days. If this seems like a cursory job, it was speeded by the obvious fact that most of the land they saw was good.

"The party again made Norton's their headquarters," Tappan continues. "After resting a day or two, and also procuring our usual supply of provisions," including the old Monongahela of course, "the party went through the 3rd Tier of Townships and returned through the Fourth Tier." This run included

Bath in which they found nothing to "equalize". In fact most of the poor land they discovered lay in swamps along the Huron River, and it was equalized with land in the townships of the 19th Range, adjoining the Firelands.

The equalizers rested up this time in Hudson, the most important community in its part of the Reserve, and stayed with David Hudson himself. They finished the job late in the fall, experiencing the magnificent weather which is the delight of northern Ohio—interrupted of course by one bad storm. After covering the remaining townships in the northern tiers the party dispersed in Cleveland. Tappan lived on for many years in Lake County, became a judge, like almost everyone else, and a postmaster in Unionville. He was one of the most useful of the early settlers in the Western Reserve.

The report of the Equalizing Committee would make interesting reading, but it has not survived. The draft of the lands west of the Cuyahoga was delayed, to the annoyance of the Company and its shareholders, until the spring of 1807 because of difficulties in completing the boundary between the Reserve and the Firelands. It was not until April 4, 1807, that a meeting was held in Hartford for the draft and the details which preceded it. There were 46 townships involved and the important "Classing Committee" had already performed its work. Its stiffly worded report was as follows:

> Your Committee appointed to Class the Proprietors according to mode of Partition in such a way as to enable them to Draw the Lands lying west of the Cuyahoga having completed the business of their appointment now Report   That they find it requires an interest of twenty six thousand eighty seven dollars of the original purchase of the State to Draw a Township or a 46th Part of the said lands as reported by the Equalizing Committee and have accordingly proceeded to Class the Proprietors into forty-six Classes and which is hereby annexed which is submitted by your Committee.
>
> Hartford, April 4, 1807
> Dan L. Coit
> Eph'm Root
> Elisha Tracy

The sum of $26,087 per township was the largest for any of the drafts, and the drawing was held the same day. In Class Six were the following proprietors with their appropriate shares:

Thomas Bull	5560
Ezekiel Williams	4800
Samuel W. Williams	4800
Timothy Burr	3000
Timothy Burr heirs	2000
Elisha Strong	4000
W. & J. Battles	1927
	26,087

In the draft, these men in Class Six drew Township 3, Range 12. For the time being, until the township could be surveyed into lots, its 14,790 acres of arable land were held in common by the six gentlemen and the heirs of Timothy Burr, who were represented, it seems, by Ephraim Root.

* * * * * *

The Bulls of Hartford were a solid, numerous family though not particularly distinguished. Captain Thomas Bull was one of the original proprietors of the town and won his army rank for service in the war against the Pequot Indians. He died in Hartford in 1684. One of his numerous great-grandsons was Captain Caleb Bull, an officer in the French and Indian Wars. He was born in 1717 and married Martha Caldwell. Typical of the enormous families which were in part the cause of the constant migration from land-poor Connecticut, the couple had seventeen children, five of whom died in infancy. Among the twelve who survived, James was born in 1751, Michael in 1763, and Thomas in 1765. Thomas married Lucinda Barbara Blake, and her name appears on the deed her husband signed with Jonathan Hale.

The three Bull brothers were "traders" or merchants with a respectable standing in the Hartford community. To judge from his correspondence, Thomas received a rather elementary education, for his penmanship, grammar, and spelling were far from perfect.

The Bull brothers became proprietors or shareholders in the Connecticut Land Company in 1796, as we have seen, with James acting at first for the three of them. Like most of the other proprietors, their investment was made principally on credit, and this made it easier for Thomas to take over the interests of James and Michael. James is not mentioned in Land Company affairs after 1796. In the drafts of 1798 and 1802, Michael and Thomas were "classed" together, but in the drawing of 1807 for the lands west of the Cuyahoga, Thomas Bull acted alone. Both his brothers were still alive and lived for years, but they may have found the business of dealing in land too risky. In fact, as far as we know, it was not notably profitable for Thomas.

Around 1807, Thomas Bull, like many other Connecticut men, put his affairs in the Western Reserve into the capable hands of Turhand Kirtland, who was already an agent for the Company and had found time to travel as an equalizer in the western townships. He may well have chosen to go because the job gave him first-hand knowledge of the quality of this land.

Some, at least, of Bull's letters to Kirtland concerning his lands have survived, though all the other half of the correspondence is lost. They give an enlightening view of the difficulties in selling land at long-range, for Thomas Bull never visited the Reserve, and they tell us much about Bull's tract in Township 3, Range 12.

The land Bull drew in Bath Township amounted to less than a fourth of his total holdings in the Reserve. All told, by draft or purchase, they added up to more than 16,500 acres, though he did not hold all of them at any one time and they were scattered from Trumbull County to Summit and Cuyahoga. They were a considerable investment, though much of it was slow in selling. In 1816, 6,137 acres, probably all Bull had left, had been mortgaged to the managers of the Connecticut School Fund, to whom the money was legally due. But he was by no means alone, for the majority of the proprietors were similarly involved.

After the draft of 1807, Bull joined in an informal partnership with Ezekiel Williams, Jr., in regard to the land they both held in Township 3, Range 12. Williams was a man of far more cultivation than Bull, as his letters to Kirtland show, and he also managed the affairs of Samuel W. Williams, his brother or perhaps a son. Bull and Williams worked with Kirtland to dispose of the property, and together they owned about 60 percent of the township, with Williams' tract lying around Ghent and Yellow Creek. Their letters to Kirtland give us a clear enough picture of what happened to Township 3, Range 12.

On May 29, 1807, before the township had been surveyed into lots, Williams wrote to Kirtland that the owners of the land had not met to discuss its survey, "but I have no doubt they will agree to have the town run out. I will thank you to give me an estimate of the expense." He went on, "if you are possessed of any information relative to the township either as to quality or its local situation which you did not communicate to Mr. Bull pray write me by the first post." Unfortunately, we do not have Kirtland's letter.

On July 21, 1807, Bull, who was always pressed for money, wrote Kirtland about the possibility of selling his share in the township even before the land was surveyed, a common practice in the speculative land deals in the Reserve. "I would not take one dollar (per acre) in the gross for it," he wrote, "but would sell at short credit at one dollar and 60 cents and for cash in hand 1.50/100. Unless Mr. Williams and myself should sell in this way we shall ere long get you to survey, etc." His chances of selling at short credit were far better than those for sale for cash, though such credit usually turned out to be long.

That fall, on October 25th, Williams wrote an interesting letter to Kirtland about the property, which had still not been surveyed:

> ... Mr. Bull, myself and the other proprietors of Township No. 3 in 12th Range have requested you to survey the same and run it out into lots of suitable size to accomodate purchasers, and in case any particular part of the township is much superior to the rest, to lay that much in smaller lots, that the partition may be made more equal. I wish you to proceed in the survey immediately that it may be com-

pleted reasonably for us to make partition so early as to give those who are inclined opportunity to commence their sales this winter—When it is finished I shall wish you [to] send with the plan the minutes from the surveyors' book as [they] will enable us to judge of the relative value—Be good enough to have it done with as much oeconomy as the business will admit.

The survey was probably made that autumn, though the copy of the field notes which has come down to us is not dated. The work was done by Rial McArthur and one R. Warden. McArthur was an experienced surveyor and was living on land he owned in adjoining Northampton. We know that the township was first divided by its owners into tracts, but none-the-less it was surveyed on the basic plan of the 160-acre lot, though rather inaccurately. This ignored Williams' suggestion for varying sizes, but the difference in quality was adjusted in terms of price.

The notes McArthur took in his field book are principally surveyors' calculations and jargon, but they do include information about the land which is important. It was this sort of thing, of course, which Williams wanted to see when he asked for the notes. For one thing, McArthur decided that most of the land was ideal for growing wheat and corn, especially wheat—and he was no doubt speaking here from his own experience with similar land in Northampton. For this reason he gave the township the name of Wheatfield, which would not be out of place today and is far more significant than Bath.

McArthur also discovered, in the northeastern part of the township in the land of the Hales and beyond, that his compass deflected while surveying the north-south lines of the lots. He wrote:

The reasons I believe for those lines being attracted are account of the vast Quantity of Iron Ore that lies in the Earth Under where those lines pass Over or near to it. There is all Appearance of Ore in the Rivulets—small pieces of which held near the needle had particular influence on it and by passing through deep hollows had had particular influence on those lines heretofore specified. There has not [been] any attraction trouble in the West half of the Town.

It was soon discovered, unfortunately, that the ore was not worth mining.

McArthur's notes also mention the quality of the land he passed through and the variety of the trees he and his axmen encountered. On the second parallel, which ran between lots 10 and 11, he found near the river "hills, full of deep gullies or gutters, and timber white oak—black oak—beech though the land (is) of an Oak quality generally." On the third parallel which bounded the Hale land on the south, he commented on that part which lay on the plateau above the valley in terms he used for much of the rest of the township. "The land fertiley level, dry wheat land—a sufficiency of moisture for grass." Considering that all this land lay in virgin timber, these remarks required shrewd and experienced observation.

Further south, in the slopes to the Valley beyond Ira Road, he found the land "hilly, knoby and thin . . . poor Rocky hills, chestnut land." Further on, "the timber is oak of both kinds (black and white) with some sugar maples." Around the north branches of Yellow Creek he found "mountains and hilly." In Lot 31, now crossed by Martin Road winding down to the Valley, he found "considerable appearance of iron ore."

For what were charmingly called "Lot Corners and their Witnesses," surveyors in these days used the larger trees, appropriately notched. In the vicinity of the Hale land McArthur lists white oak, hickories, beech, gum trees, poplars, whitethorn, and, more interesting, a large proportion of "sugar trees."

*   *   *   *   *   *

When word reached Hartford that the survey was finished, Kirtland probably having enclosed McArthur's field notes as evidence, Bull and Williams were anxious to proceed with the final partition of the township among its seven owners, including the heirs of Timothy Burr. Because of these heirs, in fact, the partition had to be authorized by the Ohio courts, and Bull asked that the "application" be made in his name and that of Ezekiel and Samuel Williams. He adds in his clumsy style, "Please to give us your opinion of the price it (the land) will bring in your first letter."

Bull writes significantly, "Cash being very scarce here, should you have any in your hand from any Contract made by me . . . will thank you to remitt it." This lack of cash, which Williams also mentions more politely, was chronic all over the country at the time, due in part to the growing difficulties with England and restrictions on trade. It was one of the reasons for Bull's financial embarrassment which led to mortgaging his land to the School Fund Managers—and for the terms of his sale of 500 acres to Jonathan Hale.

The partition of the land in Township 3, Range 12, was made sometime during the winter of 1807 and 1808, for on April 14, 1808, Bull wrote to Kirtland that the "price of eight lots in Township No. 3—12th Range I am satisfied with." We do not know who bought these, the price, or where they were. He went on, "if any lots should be worth more than what I have offered you will of course ask it—but not to put them higher than what you really think they are worth," sage advice which Kirtland scarcely needed.

Bull was now in difficulty with the School Fund people. "I expect to make a negotiation with the State," he wrote to Kirtland, "to take my land in New Connecticut and release my property they have here," meaning that he had mortgaged land in Hartford and thereabouts to the School Fund and wanted to transfer the mortgage to land in the Reserve. "I shall mention your name as one of the appraisers," of the Western land. "The amount I want to secure . . . is $12,500 of principal and I should wish to take it from that part which is least likely to sell first," a canny plan which would not have appealed to the managers of the School Fund. He adds, "as it is merely for security— I would wish to realize all I can myself at the present time and yet make the State secure." Bull was clearly in trouble. His land in the West was moving slowly and continued to do so for the next two years.

In 1809 there was further trouble with Kirtland over paying the taxes assessed by Ohio on the land west of the Cuyahoga, and Bull's relations with his agent began to cool. The economic situation in Connecticut was growing acute, thanks to the troubles with England. By the fall of 1809 both Bull and Williams were selling what land they could from Hartford, by-passing Kirtland entirely.

For this reason the partners asked Kirtland for a plan of the "Lotts" in Township 3, Range 12, for "we wish to obtain the best price we can and not prevent the sale by setting them too high," which they probably suspected Kirtland of doing. "And you know it is very difficult to judge without a map or plan of the Town—please send us one as soon as possible."

It is probable that Kirtland sent a plan of the township and that Bull or his Hartford agents showed it around the countryside to prospective buyers during the winter of 1809 and 1810. By now the lack of cash for doing business of any sort had become acute and credit was also tight. As a result, businessmen were resorting to what amounted to barter in one form or another, and both Bull and Williams were willing and eager to barter land in Ohio for land in Connecticut, which was far less of a risk and lay near at hand.

It was during these months that Jonathan Hale of Glastonbury and his brother-in-law, Jason Hammond of near-by Bolton, saw these plans. As we shall see, they were both in the market for land in the West. In April we know that Bull and Williams were both short of cash and growing worried. "I wish to crowd the sale of my lands," Bull wrote to Kirtland hastily, "and if you have any money I beg you to send it forward as Mr. Williams as well as myself want it."

Under this sort of pressure, the deals between Bull and Hale and Hammond were struck. On June 7, 1810, Bull wrote to Kirtland the only letter we have which concerns his sale of land in Township 3, Range 12, or any place else in the Reserve. By extraordinary good luck, it concerns these deals:

> "Dear Sir— I have sold to Mr. Jason Hammond in Township 3, 12th Range in the Reserve Eleven hundred Acres of Land and Also to Mr. Jonathan Hale Five Hundred Acres of the Same Town in Exchange for Property in This State—any assistance, Direction or advice given to the Bearer Mr. Theodore Hammond who is going out to the Lands will oblige
>
> Your assured friend and humble servant
>
> T. Bull

P.S. I shall Soon dispose of all my lands in this Township—Should Mr. [Theodore] Hammond meet with any misfortune on his route his Father is very able and you may rest assured will pay any Expense Should it be necessary and Wanted.

T. Bull

Theodore Hammond, who eventually delivered this letter to Kirtland, was Jason Hammond's twenty-year-old son. Before he reached Poland he needed all the "assistance, Direction or advice" both Kirtland and Jonathan Hale could give him.

The deals between Bull and Hale and Hammond had been under discussion for weeks or months, for the plans of the new settlers were ready to move. On June 11th Theodore started from Glastonbury with a wagon and a team of lumbering oxen. The following day Jonathan Hale himself, with a wagon and a team of horses, set out to overtake him on the long, hard road to the Western Reserve.

III

THE HALES OF GLASTONBURY

When Jonathan Hale whipped his team onto the flat-bottomed ferry which crossed the Connecticut River at Rocky Hill, he left behind him the rich bottom lands, the ploughed fields, pastures, and hilly woodland on the farm which had been the home of his family for five generations. It lay some eight miles south of Hartford in the town of Glastonbury on the east bank of the river. Jonathan was bound for New Connecticut, known also as the Connecticut Western Reserve.

The first of the Hales to cross the sea to New England was Captain Samuel. He was born in Hertfordshire northwest of London about 1615 and was living in the Connecticut River settlement of Hartford by 1635. Two years later he volunteered in the bloody war against the Pequot Indians, going back to Hartford with the rank of Captain. He probably moved to Wethersfield, just down the river, in 1642, for in that year he married Mary Smith, daughter of the town's minister, the Reverend Henry Smith. The young couple's second child and first son was Samuel, Junior, born in Wethersfield in 1645.

When the boy was six years old, the family moved to the new town of Norwalk where Samuel, Senior, was active in town politics. But life there was hard and he brought the family back to Wethersfield in 1660, building a house on the meadow land of the eastern shore of the river. This part of Wethersfield is now Glastonbury Town and Hales have lived there ever since.

As they settled down in Wethersfield the two Samuel Hales, father and son, bought land which was part of the first acreage in the Colony to be surveyed into farms. It was known as the Naubuc Farms and the survey was made as early as 1640. The land ran back from the Great River, as the colonists called it, just south of the Hartford town line. The terminology used in the purchase and division of these old farms shows the origin of that used by the Connecticut Land Company for similar purposes more than 150 years later. The two Samuel Hales were among the "proprietors" who bought the Naubuc Farms. The land was divided by lot, hence the term "lots" to describe a farm. Captain Samuel apparently bought three lots—or drew them. Samuel, Junior, bought one, and it was part of this which came down to the Jonathan Hale who moved his family west to the Cuyahoga in 1810.

The Naubuc lots had a curious pattern, one which was copied in other towns on the river. According to the Glastonbury town historian, the Reverend

Alonzo Chapin, "each lot was bounded by the Great River and by the wilderness East, each being three miles long. The object of this seems to have been that everyone might possess a due portion of meadow, of upland suitable for cultivation, and of woodland furnishing the fuel and timber for all necessary purposes."

This was an improvement, though a clumsy one, over the original planning of the Connecticut Valley towns. In these earlier plans pasture and woodland were often held in common by the town and its proprietors. The farm land granted a settler was usually scattered here and there within the town boundaries. As it happened, the land Jonathan bought from Thomas Bull in the Cuyahoga Valley, rather by accident—for he bought it sight unseen —supplied all these needs in one compact farm. His 500 acres contained bottom lands, meadow, and woodland.

Each of Captain Samuel's three lots was only 660 feet wide, but they lay side-by-side. Farther south along the river, the younger Samuel had one lot only 223 feet wide. How these slivers of land, running three miles back from the river, could be farmed with any sense or economy it is hard to see. Samuel, Junior, also had a strip across Wright's Island in the middle of the river which gave him valuable fishing rights. It was there and still valuable in Jonathan's time, but the meanderings of the Connecticut have now moved it east to the Glastonbury shore.

The center of each of these old Connecticut towns was its meeting house, which was in fact its church. The most powerful figure in every town was its minister, the arbiter of morals and politics, the intellectual life of his people and especially their religion. The eastern part of the town of Wethersfield, across the river, with its broad and fertile fields, was growing in population and importance, but it had no church or minister. After discussions in the Wethersfield Church and the General Court in Hartford, the eastern part was allowed to form a Congregational Society of its own in 1690. The next step was logical: the freemen east of the river petitioned the Court for the privilege of becoming a town. The town took the name of "Glastenbury", as it was spelled until the end of the nineteenth century, from an ancient seat of monastic learning in Somersetshire in the West of England.

In Chapin's report of the first town records, dated 1693, there were 34 families in the new community and six were Hales. Through marriage the Hales formed close ties with other prominent Glastonbury families we shall hear more of later on—the Welleses, who gave the Colony a Governor and Abraham Lincoln a Secretary of the Navy, the Wrights and the Talcotts.

Though the morals of the meeting house were strict, these were rough-and-tumble times as well. Trials of strength on the meeting house greens were a common and popular sport, with the victor winning the title of "Bully." The

Reverend Chapin writes that the Hales were "men of large size and uncommon strength" and that Captain Samuel was the acknowledged Bully of what was then the eastern shore of Wethersfield.

Samuel Hale, Junior, married twice. His first wife was Ruth Edwards and his second was Mary Welles, a daughter of Captain Samuel Welles the Governor's son. The oldest of Mary's four children was Jonathan, born in 1695. We shall call him Jonathan I because he became the grandfather of the Jonathan who is the principal figure in this book.

Jonathan I was the most prominent and prosperous Hale of his generation. He inherited from his father "all that Lott of Land whereon I now live," which was the strip running back from the river and including part of Wright's Island, and he also inherited land from his wealthy father-in-law. Among other things he inherited from his mother two cherished objects—a silver cup and a featherbed. He bought and sold land in the town and in his later years he paid the highest land tax in Glastonbury. He was elected to the General Court off-and-on for thirty years, served as Auditor of the Colony, and from 1739 to 1772 he was Justice of the Peace in Glastonbury. To his grandson he left an important name.

More interesting, perhaps, this Jonathan found time to be clerk of the schools in Glastonbury for thirteen years. Chapin says that his records were kept in a "clear, round hand with few peculiarities and these mainly by the substitution of *oo* for *ou* or *u,* as in *hoose, yoose, poond* . . . and the like, which he may have inherited from his parents, or acquired from the fashionable pronunciations of educated men."

Jonathan I married Sarah Talcott, of another old and prosperous local family, and the couple had eight children. The seventh was Theodore. He was born in 1735 and married another Talcott, Rachel, whose father was Colonel Elizur Talcott a distant relative of Theodore's mother.

As a young man Theodore served a brief fifteen days in a militia company commanded by his father-in-law in the French and Indian War. During the Revolution, however, Hale men saw far more active service than this. One of them was Theodore's oldest brother, another Jonathan, who died in 1776 "a few days after he returned sick from the army." It was sickness rather than enemy fire that decimated most of the armies until after the Civil War. Later Theodore served less tragically as a "member of the line" along with his older brother David and a number of Hale cousins. In plainer words they were infantrymen, the sturdy, country-bred Continentals.

Theodore and Rachel Talcott Hale had eleven children. Two of them died in infancy, another at sixteen, and a fourth at twenty-five. Jonathan was born on April 23, 1777, in the fine brick house his father and grandfather had built on the west side of what is now Main Street. He was the tenth in the family of eleven, and he and his brother Jehiel with whom he had very genial relations were the only sons to survive their father. When Jehiel married in 1795 and moved into a house of his own, the burden of the work of the farm fell on the ageing Theodore and eighteen-year-old Jonathan, with the help of occasional hired men, of course. And Theodore died in 1807.

Thus, Jonathan grew up as a farmer's son and slowly took over not only the work but the management of a long narrow lot stretching from Wright's Island across the long, level meadow land to the hills three miles away. From two invaluable account books which have luckily come down to us, we know a good deal about this Glastonbury farm of the Hales. The older of the two books was used by Theodore between 1763 and 1774, ending three years before Jonathan's birth. The second account book was Jonathan's, dated in his own hand on May 21, 1804. His last entries were made in Bath, Ohio, on July 18, 1824.

These account books and a third pertaining entirely to Jonathan's farm in the Western Reserve have unusual importance. They allow us to compare the life, the arts of farming, and much of the daily economy in Connecticut with that in the Western Reserve. But only the Glastonbury period will concern us here.

The account books prove that the Hales' relations with their hired men and a handful of local craftsmen like cobblers and woodworkers were on a barter basis—an exchange of goods and services with very little cash involved—for the reason that cash in Connecticut's history was almost always scarce. On the "credit" side of the little books, the right-hand page, are listed the chores done for the Hales or the articles they bought. Balancing on the "debit" side are the payments made by the Hales in produce or even in such services as carting or plowing. Because these entries involve only a load of wood or a bushel of rye, it seems likely that the Hales sold larger amounts of items like these which do not appear in the books. They may have been paid for in cash, or more likely by note.

From Theodore's account book we know that he cut large amounts of timber in the woodlands which climbed the gentle hills far back from the river. The principal grain crop mentioned in his accounts is "rie", as he spelled it, which was used for bread and quite likely for whiskey too. He also mentions wheat, corn, and flax, tobacco and turnips, "appels" and "sider", both usually sold by the barrel. Other produce was eggs and chickens, pork, beef, and veal, and occasionally whole or skim milk, cheese, and leather.

But the farm produced two unusual crops, thanks to the river and its rich bottom lands. One was onions, grown in the black soil which Jonathan used as a standard of comparison for the best soil he found in the Cuyahoga Valley.

In July and August "onions" were sold on "rops", or ropes, in Theodore's day at 3 pence a rope. Often more than a hundred ropes were sold at a time, and in 1774 Theodore put 200 on a sloop for shipment down the river.

The other "crop" of unusual interest was fish. By Theodore's time rights in the "fish place" on Wright's Island had grown in value and in Jonathan's they became the subject of prolonged and detailed litigation. Fish are a common entry in Theodore's book but occur very seldom in Jonathan's. It may be that Jonathan sold his catch in bulk, for we know that he fished and was skilled at building boats and making and mending nets. Only three varieties of fish are mentioned. By far the most important was shad, the "money crop", but "sammon" were common—there is a Salmon Creek in Glastonbury—and an occasional sturgeon is mentioned.

All these items were used by Theodore or Jonathan to balance their side of the account book. Jonathan also did such chores as cutting and carting timber, hoeing corn, and even fishing. He bartered vinegar, candles, hay poles, fence rails, and "keeping horses", none of which Theodore mentions.

The "credit" side of the pages shows what the Hales received in return for all these goods and services. It has a wide variety and offers the principal contrast between the life of the wilderness on the Cuyahoga and that in comparatively civilized Connecticut. There are few luxuries, unless oysters can be counted that. Two of the commonest items in the accounts of both the Hale men are rum and shoes. Theodore records in his quaint spelling that he credited Joseph Ware for "Soleing Lucy Shoes," "Maken a Pear of Shoes for Jehiel," "putting a Cap on my Shoes," and so on. Jonathan was far more literate, but he still used the convenient word "soleing."

Jonathan used the barter system to pay for far more work on his farm than his father had done; otherwise he would have been working alone. Men hired for a day or so, or even part of a day, plowed, mowed, threshed rye, made fences and window frames, broke flax, cleaned the "fish place", helped him fish when the shad were running. Skilled craftsmen did work on a different basis, for in November, 1809, Stephen Bell was given credit for $25 for "work joining on my house." This seems to refer to interior woodwork and the price, Jonathan notes, was "arranged", not charged by the day.

In the spring of 1809 one Ashbel Riley received credit for $18 for six months of "service farming." The rate of $3 a month must mean that it was part-time work. The $18 was paid, or balanced, by a list of items adding up to $14.51, Jonathan paying the rest in cash. Among the things credited to Ashbel's account was a pair of shoes for $1.34 and another "thick" pair for only $1.33, along with two charges for "mending same." Ashbel received three yards of gingham, a homemade suit, a hat, and three or four illegible items. And the list includes a "Grammar Book" assessed at 25 cents and a "Psalm

Book" at 60. None of these items was Jonathan able to supply from his farm, unless it was second hand, as no doubt some of them were.

Still another interesting item, dated December, 1807, is a credit to Ira Hubbard for "making a breakfast table" for $5.34 and a "set of Chairs & one arm chair" for $9.38. The following July, Jonathan ordered a "Bureau" for $12.00. These pieces did not travel to the Cuyahoga Valley, no doubt because they were bulky and fragile.

Hubbard, the cabinet maker, was paid in goods for the most part. He took twenty shad, a "Carvel of Cider," a load of hay and a load of wood, a whitewood panel used in making the seats for the chairs, fifty fence rails, and something far more significant, 2,200 bricks valued at $12.28. There was also a credit of $1.50 for carting the brick.

We know that Theodore and his father, Jonathan I, made the bricks they used to build the house in which Jonathan II was born. It still stands, in sturdy good repair, on Main Street not far from the center of the modern town. Legend has it that the clay came from across the road, though there is no evidence to prove it now. There are only scattering references to brick in Theodore's accounts, but Jonathan made an important business out of it, particularly in the last years of his life in Glastonbury. In 1808 he made at least 5,200 brick and sold them for what seems the unprofitable price of $29.28. Some of this is described as "weathered", for exterior use, and some as "soft", for use inside. It is safe to say that he made far more brick than this, for his customers must have included men of substance who would not be likely to pay in barter.

In October, 1809, Jonathan apparently built a new kiln. He hired Captain Abraham Tallcott and Charles Williams to work three days each "setting (a) brick kiln." The Captain was the foreman, for he was paid $2.25 while Williams got only $2.00. Both men were paid largely with wood. In March, 1810, three months before he set out for the Western Reserve, Jonathan sold 2,100 soft brick to Abel Lewis for $6.00, just about half his price for weathered.

*   *   *   *   *   *

Jonathan attended the old Town School of which his grandfather had been clerk. Like the church, it was held in the Meeting House. One thing about his education is clear: from the evidence of the account books kept by his father and himself, Jonathan's training was more thorough than Theodore's in matters of spelling and grammar, though far from perfect. His penmanship is that of a man who wrote rather frequently, while for Theodore it was obviously an occasional effort. The letters we have in Jonathan's hand are surprisingly literate for a man who could not have had more education than was available in the Town School of Glastonbury. Later on we will quote from these interesting letters and also give samples of the verse he wrote.

In Jonathan's day the church was almost as important as school in the life
of a boy. As far as we know, the Glastonbury "Society", as the Congregational
churches were called, was sensibly orthodox. During the middle eighteenth
century the church in New England had been torn by theological conflict, but
this had subsided in the days of the Revolution. The Sunday sermons Jonathan
heard were long, in morning and afternoon sessions, and the standard fare was
what seems today like impossibly intricate theological argument. Jonathan
remained a Congregationalist all his life, but for us the most interesting aspect
of his church-going was his absorbing interest in music and the choir.

This music has an interesting history in Glastonbury. For many years
after the settlement of New England, church music, simple at best, was "tradi-
tionary", that is, it was a matter of local custom and the familiar hymns and
the method of singing them, even the words, varied from town to town.
Around 1712, a movement began in the church to teach a standard form of
singing and to write down the notes of the hymns. Oddly, this sensible plan
aroused a storm, particularly in Massachusetts, for the people had become
attached to "singing by note" rather than "singing by rule."

In Glastonbury, the Reverend Chapin writes, "the matter was quietly and
easily disposed of by a vote of the town in February, 1733, directing the congregation . . . to sing one-half of the day by 'note' and the other half by 'rule'."
However, instruction had to be given in singing by rule, and the Church
required its members to meet at sessions in the Meeting House and in private
homes in various parts of the town. One of these regular meetings was held once
a week in the "Hoose of Jonathan Hale," our Jonathan's grandfather. Mr.
Chapin concludes, "The idea of singing without learning, or of being excused
from making an effort to learn, seems never to have entered the minds of our
ancestors." It was this solid practice and tradition of musical schooling which
came down to Jonathan from his grandfather's day. It is probable that Theodore sang in the Meeting House choir and we have proof that two of Jonathan's
older brothers did. For Jonathan took with him to the Cuyahoga Valley a
hymn book which Samuel Hale bought in 1795, three years before his early
death, and another which was the gift of Jehiel Hale, who had acquired it in
1791. However, Jonathan's interest in singing and in teaching choirs to sing,
was far more a part of his life in the Western Reserve than in Connecticut.
We shall return to it later.

But there are other aspects of Jonathan's love of music. One of them was
the writing of "tunes." We know about this from some delightful letters
Jonathan received from his nephew Joseph Wright while he was a student at
Yale. Joseph was the son of James Wright whose family gave its name to the
"fishing place", and of Jonathan's sister Lucy. He was seven years younger

than his uncle. In the early years, at least, their long relationship was close, and in these youthful letters Joseph gives it an amusing intellectual air.

The earliest surviving letter which Joseph wrote to his uncle is written in a naively formal prose which vanished in later letters. It was written from Yale College on November 18, 1803, the year before Joseph graduated.

"You will recollect, undoubtedly," he wrote, "that a short conversation subsisted between you and myself, some time since, respecting the making our effort in production of a song or tune; we alloting the former part of the labour to me, the latter to yourself." He explained at some length that he had had no time to devote to the project until now. "I have completed a few rhymes which I would without arrogance or pride submit to you to be sett to a tune of yours." The first and last of the four stanzas serve as adequate samples of the rest:

> Musick! a sweet, a lovely friend
> Whose voice will e'er true taste attend.
> What pow'rful mover does she prove
> Of minds, to seek her but to love.

> ————

> But when to noblest use thou'rt come,
> When praises she gives to Father, Son,
> How does her pow'r, her sweetness shine,
> How great the pleasure, how divine.

We do not know whether Jonathan ever wrote this tune, but we do know that he sent Joseph at least one from Ohio. Composing such simple melodies was clearly a hobby of his.

Joseph's later letters show that their mutual interest in music continued. On January 7, 1806, Joseph wrote from New Haven that he was enclosing a "number of marches, airs, etc. which if they contribute to enliven your leisure hours I shall receive ample recompence for my pains."

Three weeks later Joseph wrote that this letter and its contents had not been acknowledged, but Jonathan was always a slow correspondent. Joseph goes on to say that he had attended a musical in New Haven "where the dulcet tones of a female singer charmed me." Then he adds, "Your harmonious voice, however, would have added dignity to the choir." This sort of cultivated flattery was common in his mature letters, mostly on legal matters, though often Joseph's irritation at Jonathan's delays in answering questions clearly shows through.

We know from many sources that Jonathan played the violin, and the scores Joseph sent him may have been arranged for that purpose or possibly for singing. But this broad interest in music and the fact that he was able to indulge it in Glastonbury, with its Calvinist inheritance, shows that many of the old taboos had vanished. And one wonders where he learned to play the violin.

On July 11, 1802, at the age of twenty-five, Jonathan married Mercy Piper, who was two years younger. Mercy's parents were Samuel and Olive Adams Piper, from comparatively humble stock. Samuel was a tailor by trade and his wife may have been one too. Mercy herself, we know, was trained as a "tailoress" and made clothes for gentlemen, compared to the "seamstress" who made them for ladies. While this placed the Pipers at a lower social level than the Hales, Mercy's skill came in handy in Connecticut and even more so in the Western Reserve.

Mercy was born in Acton, Massachusetts, in 1779. The following year the family moved south to the part of Glastonbury Town known as Eastbury. Samuel had six children by Olive Adams and after her death he married again and his second wife bore him eleven more. Of Olive's six children three were boys, for Jonathan corresponded with two of Mercy's brothers, Samuel and Luther—the latter hardly a Calvinist name—and a third, Josiah, who moved to Bath, lived with the Hales and did chores for Jonathan. Samuel Piper seems to have moved to Cleveland in the 1820s. Jonathan's marriage to Mercy can hardly compare with the earlier family ties with the Welleses, Talcotts, and Wrights. There can be no doubt that it was a love affair, for it could scarcely have furthered Jonathan, financially or socially.

Mercy's humble birth, with the hardships and household chores it must have involved, was an asset to her family in the Western Reserve. A woman of more elegant background and less useful accomplishments might not have put up with the log cabin Mercy managed so well for fifteen years. In fact it is probable that most of the women of the higher strata, wives or daughters of the great proprietors, settled more comfortably in places like Canfield, Warren, or Poland, and later in Hudson, Stow and Tallmadge. O. W. Hale, Mercy's grandson, wrote that "her sons testify to her kind heartedness, her bravery, her fortitude, her self-denial she so often practiced for the sake of her husband and children, and the great tact she had for overcoming the privations of pioneer life."

In Glastonbury Mercy quite naturally developed a small clientele for the gentlemen's clothes she had been taught to cut and sew. There are entries for her work recorded in Jonathan's account book from its earliest pages, listing the coats, "jacets", and pantaloons she made for neighbors or such prosperous relations as the family of James Wright. For James, in fact, she altered "a great coat for Rebecca" who seems to have been his sister. This is typical of the contrast between the leisurely life of Glastonbury and that of the Western Reserve; in the former Mercy usually charged for "cutting and making" garments, in the latter she more frequently "cut" and the frontier wife did the sewing, as we shall see.

Theodore Hale died in 1807, leaving his widow Rachel and seven children to divide his estate. It was valued in an inventory at $7,622.19, a sizable sum for the times, but more than half of it was invested in the farm. In his will Theodore left "one half of the homestead" to his eldest son, Jehiel, who had married and had a house of his own. To Jonathan, his only other surviving son, who was living with Mercy in the old brick house, he left "part of the homestead", apparently the remaining half. From later evidence, as we shall see, Jonathan seems to have inherited the original ribbon of farm running three miles back from the river, though it amounted to only 100 acres.

To his five daughters Theodore left gifts of money, after the custom of the time and with a careful eye on the married state of each of them. Rachel, the oldest child, was married to Jason Hammond, who figures in a most important way in this story. Jason was a farmer, miller, and merchant in Manchester, a town just east of Hartford, and in 1803 he had inherited 116 acres of farmland in neighboring Bolton from his father. He also owned one or two ships engaged in the West Indies trade, but the Embargo of 1807—the year Theodore died—had locked the ships in Connecticut harbors. He had bought most of his merchandise for the store in Manchester and for overseas trade from a relative, Colonel Abijah Hammond, in New York City, and the Embargo had apparently ruined them both. It was perhaps for this reason that Theodore left to Rachel the rather sizable sum of sixteen pounds, ten shillings, and three pence, which may have come out even in terms of the dollars which were used in actual exchange in Connecticut.

Lucy Hale, as we know, had married a prosperous farmer and neighbor, James Wright, and her father left her the nominal sum of five shillings. To his unmarried daughters, Ruth, Sarah, and Abigail, he left eighty pounds each as a sort of dowry, and the right to live in the family home until they were married. Shortly after, Sarah married her cousin Elijah Hale, and we will have a great deal to say about her and her family in later chapters of this book. At the time Jonathan and Mercy left Glastonbury for the Western Reserve, Ruth and Abigail were living at home with their mother, who was given the right to live in the house for the rest of her life.

We also know that Jonathan received from his father, probably before the latter's death, a tenth of a share in the fishing rights on Wright's Island. This gift was the cause of litigation it is impossible to follow in detail here. But it is clear that Jonathan sold half of his rights in 1810 before he left for the West, turning over the remaining twentieth of a share to his mother during her life. An "execution" was taken in the local courts against these rights in 1811, to satisfy claims against notes Jonathan had generously but unwisely endorsed for friends. But by 1826 he had somehow or other regained a twentieth of a share, that held by his mother, for in this year his brother-in-law, James

Wright, wrote to Hale about its purchase. To clarify things, Wright asked Jonathan to put in writing "that your father gave you the fish place,—that you and your associates," no doubt men who owned other shares on the island, "built the boats, nets, etc. . . . and that you sold half your share and left the other half to your mother." The next year James Wright bought Jonathan's twentieth of a share for $50.

Writing many years later, Jonathan's grandson, O. W. Hale, discussed the reasons his grandfather left Glastonbury for the Western Reserve. "Jonathan Hale's father" he wrote, "having died and leaving only a small estate to be divided between so many children—and becoming somewhat involved in debt by being surety for other parties, he became dissastified and concluded to 'Go West.' As he expressed it, he did not care to remain there and be at the 'tail of the heap'."

Similar thoughts were also occurring to Jonathan's brother-in-law and cousin, Elijah Hale, and to another and far more aggressive brother-in-law, Jason Hammond. Elijah had become even more deeply involved than Jonathan in notes he had endorsed for friends, and most of whatever he owned in Glastonbury was at stake. As we have seen, Jason Hammond had lost his prosperous business thanks to the Embargo of 1807 and he was apparently reduced to farming the 116 acres he owned in Bolton, just northeast of Glastonbury. The economic depression which was the result of the growing troubles with England and of restrictions on trade was felt most deeply in New England, and it was at the root of the financial problems which beset all three of the men.

Migration was nothing new in Connecticut. From the very earliest days of the Colony its farmers had been moving West and North in search of more and better land. In more recent years they had settled in Western Massachusetts, New Hampshire, Vermont, and the Hudson Counties of New York. Connecticut had claims on almost half of northern Pennsylvania, set up the Susquehanna Company to exploit it, and thousands of its people had settled there. Among them were the settlers in Wyoming Valley who were massacred by the Indians. After the Revolution, Connecticut people began to move west into the Mohawk Valley and then, as we know, into the Western Reserve. Migration was the old and established solution for overpopulation, poor soil, and economic ills like those which haunted Jonathan and Elijah Hale, and Jason Hammond.

It was in this frame of mind, in the winter and spring of 1810, that Jonathan, Elijah, and Jason saw the maps of Township 3, Range 12, in the Western Reserve of Connecticut which were in the possession of Thomas Bull or one of his agents. It seems likely that Jason Hammond was an acquaintance of Bull for they had both been "traders." And it is likely too that Hammond, by far more experienced in matters of business than the other two, and fifteen years older than Jonathan, was the leader in the entire affair.

As we know, Thomas Bull and his partner Ezekiel Williams were also caught in the economic depression and were eager to dispose of as much of their land in the Reserve as they could and on almost any terms. Those Jonathan and Jason agreed upon with Thomas Bull were for the exchange of their lands in Connecticut for 500 and 1100 acres respectively in Ohio. On June 7, 1810, Bull wrote explaining this to his agent in Ohio, Turhand Kirtland of Poland. Elijah Hale did not buy or exchange any land for the simple reason that he had no money or land to dispose of.

The Hales and Hammonds were so far advanced in their plans to leave, which can only mean that the transaction had been virtually settled many weeks before June 7th, that Bull's letter was given to Theodore Hammond to be delivered in person to Kirtland. As we have seen, Theodore left Glastonbury on the 11th.

However, there is one strange transaction in all this which is difficult to explain. This is a deed of sale between Jonathan and Samuel Welles. It was signed in Hartford on June 5, 1810, two days before Bull wrote his letter to Turhand Kirtland. In the deed no amount of money is mentioned. Jonathan merely agreed to "sell and confirm" to Samuel Welles "a certain piece of land where I now dwell containing about one hundred acres with the buildings thereon. Bounding north on land belonging to Gideon Hale Jno', Rev. William Lockwood, and heirs of Joseph Mosely deceased. East on a highway at the East end of the three mile lot"—which is our evidence for assuming that Jonathan's property extended that far. "South by land of Elisha Hale, Zephaniah H. Smith, Chauncey Goodrich and Jonathan Bidwell. West on Connecticut River or land of James Wright. With the encumbrance of my Mother Rachel Hale's right of dower and some other encumbrance of my two sisters Ruth and Abigail Hale having a right in the house and garden and fire wood as may be seen in the will of my father Theodore Hale deceased. Also the highway called the street and the Hartford and New London Turnpike Road running across said land."

Quite possibly Jonathan did this to free his land, or Thomas Bull, of any claims against it due to the notes he had signed, and it had been agreed that Samuel Welles, a distant relative, was to turn the land in his own name over to Bull. At any rate it gives us the only description we have of the land Jonathan owned in Glastonbury. And we know that Jonathan's deal with Bull went through, for several days after signing this curious deed he was on the road to the West.

Plans for the little exodus were made by all three of the Hale and Hammond families involved. Theodore, representing his father Jason Hammond, was to go on ahead with a team of oxen. Jonathan, carrying his personal needs and a supply of tools like the axes he would use to clear the land, was to follow. They were to examine the land, it seems, and send back a report to Jason and Elijah who would then follow along with the families if the report was good.

There was sense to this, for the families were large and there was no reason to move them west until the prospects there were known. Theodore was twenty, the oldest of all the children, while Jonathan was the youngest of the three men. Mercy and Jonathan had three young children, all born in the family home—Sophronia in 1804, William in 1806, and Pamelia in 1808. Sarah and Elijah's were ten and six years old, and the four other Hammond children ranged from nineteen to twelve. Before they arrived in the West, it was assumed that Theodore and Jonathan, if all went well, would have provided some sort of quarters in which they could live. It was a sensible plan and, as it turned out, worked very well.

IV

THE JOURNEY WEST
June - July, 1810

"This day I started," Jonathan Hale wrote in his diary on the night of June 12, 1810, "leaving family & Friends in my native town for new Connecticut. Rainy weather. No remarkable occurences, in good health, etc." He had stopped at Mr. Lewis' Tavern in Farmington where the bill was $1.00.

Every night on the long trip West, Hale jotted down notes like these in his diary, mentioning the inn or house he stayed in, and almost without fail, the amount he paid there. He was a careful, Connecticut man with money, as we know from his account books. He drove a good team of horses which stood the rough trip without trouble, and his wagon was a sturdy, square-built job, less rakish in design and smaller than the famous Conestogas of a few years later. Though it broke down a couple of times, this was no wonder in view of some of the roads he traveled. It probably had a canvas top and beneath it Jonathan had two chests and at least two boxes. They held his personal belongings and the basic tools he would need in the wilderness. The chests are now on display in the brick house he built in the Valley. The household goods were to come with Mercy, Elijah, and the Hammonds in the fall. But he undoubtedly had with him his violin and used it to while away the evenings in the taverns he stopped at along the road.

Jonathan was not planning to travel alone, for he was to catch up with young Theodore Hammond before they reached the Hudson River. Theodore drove a slow-moving yoke of oxen and a wagon filled with the same sort of items Jonathan carried. As we know, he had with him too the important letter from Thomas Bull addressed to Turhand Kirtland in Poland, informing him of the sale of land in Township 3, Range 12, to Jonathan Hale and Jason Hammond. Theodore had left Glastonbury the day before Jonathan.

The route Hale chose for his trip was the most unusual thing about it. Off hand one would have expected him to use the well-known Mohawk turnpike from Albany west, or even the famous route through Bedford in Pennsylvania. Instead he took a more direct route through the Catskills and a corner of Pennsylvania into the "southern tier" of New York State, then slanted up through the Finger Lake country to Geneva and along the Genesee Road to Buffalo. It was a far better road than the Pennsylvania route, as contemporary evidence proves, and shorter than the Mohawk road. He probably learned about it from his Uncle Elizur Talcott, who had moved to Owego on the Susquehanna in New York, and with whom he spent a long weekend on the way.

Hale traveled for 28 days, not including those he spent in Owego, and by his own calculation he covered 646 miles, probably somewhat more. This was an average of at least 23 miles a day. With a wagon, an ambling team of horses, and roads which in places was extremely bad, this was excellent time. On a few days he made 30 miles and once he made 35.

Connecticut had excellent roads for the time, according to the reliable English traveler, John Melish. In fact they were responsible in part for the complaints of Connecticut travelers on the journey west, for they found few roads as good. Hale made good time through the hills of the western part of the State, though he found "uneven country, rocks and stones." The second night he stopped at Litchfield "at Mr. Cook's at the Jail," where he "fared very well" for $1.03. Beyond Litchfield the next day, however, he lost his way, going north to Milton on a side road that was "20 degrees worse than any road I ever saw," though he was to find far worse. He turned south to Kent on the Housatonic where he stayed at Phelpses for only 50 cents lodging. From here he crossed the Taconics into New York, reaching Fishkill "10 miles from the landing" on the Hudson, on his fourth day from Glastonbury. Here he stayed with a Mr. Weeks for 74 cents the night.

At the Newburgh crossing of the North River, as Hale called the Hudson, he learned that Theodore had gone on ahead. In a letter he wrote to Mercy from Owego, Jonathan explained rather vaguely what had happened. It seems there were two ferries at Newburgh and that Jonathan crossed on the upper one, Theodore somewhat earlier on the lower one. The ferry cost him $1.92 and Jonathan complained emphatically in his diary that it was an *"enormous price."* On the Newburgh side Jonathan received word that Theodore had waited awhile "but on the whole thought he would go on," leaving his uncle a letter at the lower ferry which no doubt explained his plans. Jonathan assumed that they would meet on the road and did not bother to pick up the letter. But Theodore crossed the Catskill by a southern route and went on through Pennsylvania, where he ran into trouble, as we shall see.

In Newburgh Hale picked up the turnpikes which were to carry him, over good roads and bad, almost to Buffalo. Turnpikes are a neglected chapter in the history of American travel. Connecticut had had them for years, but in New York the first was built from Albany west around 1800. They were built by the sale of stock to farmers and merchants along the routes, and they were actually improvements on more casual existing roads and tracks.

The best known of these pikes today is the Genesee Road from Utica west, which was not completed to Buffalo until after the War of 1812. With toll gates every ten miles, according to the terms of its charter it was to be

six rods in width . . . cleared of all timber excepting trees of ornament, and to be improved in the following manner, to wit, in the
middle of the said road there shall be formed a space not less than 24
feet in breadth, the center of which shall be raised 15 inches from
the sides, rising toward the middle by gradual arch, 20 feet of which
shall be covered with gravel or broken stones, 15 inches deep in the
center and 9 inches deep on the sides, so as to form a firm and even
surface.

Few of the pikes met such specifications, but they were vital arteries of
commerce and travel. Later many were surfaced with macadam and survive as
highways today. The pikes over which Jonathan Hale drove his wagon were
probably more like the one in northern Pennsylvania—the Cochecton and
Great Bend—which the historian of Susquehanna County says was constructed
"twenty feet wide at a cost of $1,620 per mile; the materials were earth, stone,
lime, and timber. Its form was convex, being four inches higher in the center
than at the sides." It was begun in 1806 and completed the year after Hale
drove over it, and it had paid for itself before it was finished. It was over
pikes like these that Hale made the best time of his journey, and the fact
that they bridged most of the streams and swamps was as important as anything else.

Tolls varied from pike to pike, but the usual charge was 12½ cents every
ten miles for a rig like Hale's. A cart with two oxen cost only 8 cents, a
"score" of cattle cost 6 cents, and sheep or hogs only 3 cents. But a coach or
a four-wheeled carriage cost a quarter and a one-horse carriage 12¼ cents.
Clearly the tolls encouraged commerce, with the luxury trade paying the
heaviest part of the bill.

Across the southern Catskills, Hale followed the Newburgh and Cochecton
Turnpike, incorporated in 1801 as the first route to the West built after the
Mohawk pike. It was a well traveled road which opened the counties of the
southern tier to commerce and immigration. Seventeen miles from Newburgh,
Hale stopped at a "tavern on top of a hill" and "fared extremely well. Bill
$1.00." The next morning he passed through Mankating Hollow and "went
on nearly thirty miles" around White Lake, but he had to put up at an old
Scotchman's where he had "tuff Times. Bread and milk for Supper. Bill
83 cents."

This was the luck of the road. There were plenty of taverns, or at least
private houses, in which he could buy a meal and spend the night, but they
varied widely in what they could offer. On only two or three of his 28 days
on the road did Hale have to hunt for one. The best were of brick or wood
with public rooms—in the eastern part of the journey at least—but many
were mere log cabins and occasionally in the West he slept on the floor. No
doubt because they were more expensive, Hale avoided the well-known taverns

in the towns he passed through. Instead of stopping in Geneva, for instance, where the inns were good, he stopped six miles out of town. He was a country man, and in his diary he mentions now and again the state of the country and crops, but unlike other travelers of the period he says almost nothing about the towns he passed through.

On June 18th, Hale crossed the Delaware at Cochecton, a town which has all but vanished, onto the pike across the northeastern corner of Pennsylvania, "up hill and down, up hill and down, etc. I stopt at the Turnpike gate, paid 45 cents toll." This was the whole route of some 45 miles apparently, and, oddly, it was one of the few times he mentioned tolls at all, though he must have paid them often along the way. Then he "traveled in the Evening thro the woods. I finally found a tavern but no horse keeping under the hill. Bill 30 cents."

The next day he reached the unfinished part of the Cochecton and Great Bend Turnpike and covered only twenty miles. "Mud and stones up hill & down," he complained. "The worst that was ever travelled in." But at Potter's that night he "fared very well, horse keeping, supper, etc. 81 cents." The following day he struggled "on thro what is called the Beach Woods. Part the way Turnpike, but where it is not tis most Horable road." From that time on, the Beech Woods road became his standard for comparison. "I then crossed the Susquehanna River," onto the Great Bend and Bath Turnpike which followed the river valley through Binghamton and beyond, paying a toll of 25 cents. Stopping at Mr. Trowbridge's, "oats & hay, Lodgings and Bitters Cost 87 cents." The "bitters" was the whiskey Hale used on his journey with an occasional rum sling, and prescribed for Mercy as well when she came West. He believed, with reason, that most of the drinking water along the way was unsafe.

He passed through Binghamton the next day, which he called "Shenango" from the river which joins the Susquehanna there. Further on "the iron comes off my axletree. Cost 37 cents. Wheel down and old negro come along and helped me put it on." That night at Mr. Avery's he fared very well again, including bitters, but for $1.25, the most he paid for a night's lodging on the entire trip. Oddly, he made no complaint. The following day, Friday, June 22nd, he "went on to Owego and arrived at my Uncle Tallcott's about 12 o'clock," noon. "Very gratefully received," he quaintly adds.

*   *   *   *   *   *

Elizur Talcott was a brother of Jonathan's mother. Jonathan was also related, through the Talcotts, to the Goodriches who lived in Owego. The town in 1810 was prospering in a small way from the river-boat traffic up and down the Susquehanna. It had grain and saw mills, and the *New York Gazeteer* for 1813 says the population of the township was more than a thousand. On the Saturday after his arrival there, Jonathan unloaded his wagon "and went to the blacksmith & got two bands on the wheel and the axel tree fixt the whole very poorly done." It had to be done again further on. "Cost me 54 cents."

On Sunday, of course, Jonathan went "to Meeting and heard a sermon on the doctrines of the Election which much displeased many of his"—the minister's—"hearers, particularly Mr. Goodrich." He stayed on through Monday and visited Mr. Matson and Mr. Goodrich, "was treated very handsomely, dined at Capt. Eliakin Goodrich and likewise visited Doctor Jones." Most of these people probably had close ties with Glastonbury, but they had other interests in common with Jonathan, for "we had some very good music & in the Evening he," apparently Dr. Jones, "visited me at my Uncle Tallcott's where we sang until Eleven o'clock, etc." No doubt Jonathan also played his fiddle.

That day Jonathan paid "for Handkerchief 1.00", which seems very high, "for Letter paper 25 & for some other affairs 25 more so my Money goes." According to the entries in his diary the trip so far had cost him $13.86, but he had obviously skipped some of his expenses along the way, including tolls. He used the letter paper to write to Mercy the first of the four letters he sent her before the rest of the Hale and Hammond families left Glastonbury that fall. It is dated June 25th in Owego. It reads in part:

> Dear Wife
>
> I arrived here on the 22nd at my Uncle Tallcott's after a journey of ten days and a half. My journey has been very uncomfortable in a great measure by the badness of the roads. The turnpike from Newburgh is tolerably good the greater part of the way until you get to what is called the Beach Woods in Pennsylvania, where the road is not finished, five or six miles from any house thro a dreary wilderness where there is bears and wolves, deer and Catamounts very frequently seen and traveling in unknown country on a rocky, stony hilly stubby road and in the night. I've frequently wished myself at the desired haven.

As we shall see, this section of the road made a deep and unhappy impression on him. Then follows the passage concerning Theodore Hammond's change in plans, quoted above. The letter ends with a paragraph which shows Jonathan's deep religious feeling and his devotion to his wife and family:

> You must not think that my heart is far away from you, if I am absent. To leave my wife and children, Mother and sisters, friends and connections has been next to death to me, to part with, but may God grant that this may not be an everlasting parting. Though I am separated from my friends and connections, yet I have the same God to go to as you have, and may none of us fail of the blessed portion that this world can never give nor take away. My heart is full. I cannot write—silence must give you an adequate feeling by your own experience. Your affectionate and loving husband.
>
> Jno^a Hale

A postscript relates to business matters, mostly the collection of debts. "Collect in the debts you can," Jonathan writes, and then adds, "and save what money that is possible, but make yourself comfortable." This seems to have been Jonathan's policy throughout his life—to save what he could but to make himself, and particularly his family, comfortable. In this he succeeded.

The turnpike from Owego to Ithaca on Lake Cayuga had not been completed. Though Hale covered twenty-four miles the first day out from Owego, he found "a bad road some part of the way," most of it through woods. He stayed at Mr. Rowe's a few miles south of Ithaca, where he was "handsomely treated. I got my waggon fixt again paid 25 cents." The next day he "went on again thro a very bad road, thro stubs and roots, very bad traveling rain in the morning & very warm." This was a road of the true frontier, half-way between a track for Indians or a man on horseback, and a turnpike for wagon traffic. The trees had been cut and that was all. Hale covered only twenty miles that day, as he had done in the Beech Woods country. Passing the head of Lake Cayuga, he went through Ithaca, a town of some twenty houses, but does not mention the place.

The Ithaca and Geneva Turnpike was in far better shape and Hale made far better time, after stopping the night in Ulysses. "At Landlord McLalland's treated very handsomely, bill, supper and breakfast, horsekeeping, etc., 92 cents. A very good road," he adds with relief and for the first time on his trip. The following day he went on "thro a very fine country, the Wheat looks the Best of any that I have seen. This Land lies between lakes Cuyuga and Seneca. I went as far as a Tavern six miles this side of Geneva where I put up." It was called the Lake Tavern and the fare was "very indifferent." He traveled thirty miles that day, no doubt in fine weather after the rain.

From this point on, most of the way to Buffalo Creek, Hale traveled along the Genesee Turnpike, more commonly called The Great Road. He made excellent time for the next few days, in striking contrast to Theodore's experience and the reports of travelers on roads further south. For example, Margaret Dwight, a well-born Connecticut girl on her way to Warren, crossed the mountains of Pennsylvania with a party of friends that fall. While their wagon lumbered up and down six ranges of mountains on the road through Bedford, she and her companions were forced to walk much of the way to spare their exhausted horses. While Jonathan Hale averaged about thirty miles a day in New York, Margaret's party made nine or ten in Pennsylvania.

The beautiful Finger Lakes country was more settled than any Jonathan had seen since he left Connecticut, and Lake Seneca at Geneva charmed him. He wrote in his diary on June 29th:

I started from the Lake Tavern and went on to Genave where I got two Bushels of Oats for 3/1 per bus. Oats I find to be very scarce.

I cannot buy a peck of oats at a Tavern under 25 cents. This lake looks like the Long Island Sound. The wind affect [it] as much, the water looks as clear . . . I think this is to be a most Excellent Country, the roads are dry as an ash heap. Rain very much wanted. Corn & wheat looks extremely well, etc.

Many a western traveler stopped for keeps in this delightful country as he passed through it, and it obviously tempted Hale. He traveled that day through Canandaigua, which he does not mention but other travelers found attractive, staying at Landlord Watson's where again he fared well, for only 87½ cents. The next day he passed through "some very handsome towns," the only ones he praised in this way, perhaps because they reminded him of Connecticut. Among them was "Goshen," probably Geneseo, where he stopped for breakfast and "bated my horse" for 40 cents. He had picked up the custom which other travelers followed of stopping for breakfast, probably late in the morning. This is evidence again that taverns were growing in number along these western roads.

The finished turnpike dwindled away in Western New York and Hale wrote that "the road is not very good it is made with logs a considerable part five or six miles." He traveled over more of this kind of road the following day, a "very rough road chiefly made with logs, etc." This was a corduroy road, and they were not built on an extensive scale for some years. This one crossed swamp land in the Genesee valley, for Hale continues: "This day I crossed the Genesee River on a bridge that was like to fall down and then went on thro Indian settlements," called the Big Tree Reservation, "and what is called Genesee flats. . . . Traveled this day 35 miles." This was the most he covered in a single day, or mentioned in his diary.

That night, Saturday, June 30th, Hale stopped at a post office which was "just at the edge of the Holland purchase," perhaps the present town of Wyoming. The Purchase was an enormous tract in Western New York which had been bought as a speculation by a group of Amsterdam capitalists. Sometime during the day Hale met up with a man named Aaron Miller. General Lucius Verus Bierce, a crony of Jonathan in later years, tells the story in his history of Summit County. Miller was on foot and had a "bag on his back, containing meat, bread and oats—provisions for himself and family and horse. He was followed by his wife on horseback, with a little boy up behind her. On coming up a conversation ensued which I cannot give better than in Mr. Hale's own words:"

"Says the footman to Mr. Hale, 'Where mout you be going, stranger?' "
" 'To Ohio' ".
" 'I swan', says he, 'I am going there too. What part of Ohio, stranger?' "
" 'To Town three, Range twelve.' "

" 'I swan,' says he, 'So am I.' "

" 'I said to him, I have the second choice in the Bull tract in that township.' "

" 'Then I swan, you will be going right into my house—For I have got the best house in Wheatfield. I hewed the logs and split the floor from an ash log.' "

Aaron Miller was a squatter, but he was not on Jonathan's land at all. He had settled instead on Lot 10, just to the north of Jonathan's Lot 11, and the error was due to the fact that the survey lines were vague until the land was cleared. But squatting was common practice on the frontier and Miller had no sense of doing wrong. Things worked out very well and the families became close friends in the Valley.

The Millers went along with Hale for at least the following day, Mrs. Miller and the boy no doubt riding in the wagon. This was Sunday and Jonathan apologized in his diary for traveling on the Sabbath. He went on "out of necessity," he wrote that night, "or rather for the sake of Mr. Miller's company because I am unacquainted with the road. Traveled on to Vandenverters," a place a few miles east of Buffalo. Here he was "poorly provided and must say the poorest tavern I found on my Journey."

Aaron Miller is not mentioned again in the diary until Hale reached his destination. He somehow managed to make better time than Hale and reached the Cuyahoga first. Possibly he went by ship from Buffalo Creek, for the next day Hale wrote that he "went to Buffaloe a pretty good road," and at Buffalo Creek he "put one chest and two boxes aboard vessel freight $3.25." To lighten his load in this way was a wise move, for the roads from Buffalo west were the worst he coped with. But he ran a risk by trusting his belongings to the little ships of the time. On his way east along the lake shore the following year, John Melish "passed a creek, in the mouth of which lay a crazy little boat, which was bound up the lake, but could not proceed, the materials of a *moving family* were scattered abroad upon the beach."

As usual Hale passed through Buffalo without putting up at a tavern there. Melish, however, was impressed by the place, which "had been laid out for a town about five years ago and is regularly disposed in streets and lots." Its population in 1811 was about 500, larger than any town in the Reserve, and "is rapidly increasing. The buildings are mostly of wood painted white, but there is a number of good brick houses and some few of stone." It had four taverns, and a brand new weekly newspaper. "Upon the whole," Melish said with admirable foresight, "I think it is likely to become a great settlement."

*   *   *   *   *   *

On Monday night, July 2nd, Hale stayed at a tavern on the far side of Buffalo Creek, where he had "poor horsekeeping and lay on the floor," meaning, of course, no beds. He had spent 25 cents for "ferriage" across the Creek, where the following year Melish found a bridge being built, and 54 cents for his keep, such as it was. At this crude little tavern, or perhaps someplace in Buffalo, a Mr. Johnson joined Hale. He came from Westmoreland, New Hampshire, and he had a box "of goods which he wants me to carry to Grand River, in New Connecticut," Hale wrote in his diary a few days later. For some odd reason the matter had slipped his mind when he wrote in his diary at the tavern on Buffalo Creek. Johnson was a useful companion on the lonely road, and as it turned out he more than paid the expense Hale was put to in shipping part of his goods by the Lake.

From Buffalo Creek to Cleveland the road Hale traveled is difficult to trace, but by-and-large it probably followed the present Route 20, at least into Ashtabula. As early as 1798, the Connecticut Land Company had appointed a committee which "recommended the laying out and cutting of a road from Pennsylvania to the city of Cleveland at $2,600." This involved more cutting than laying, and for years it was merely a horsepath hacked through the woods. Three years later the problem of bringing settlers into the northern part of the Reserve became serious, and the Company authorized the Directors "to procure a road from Buffalo Creek to Presque Isle," or Erie, "and from thence to the East line of the Reserve so as to meet the road already cut upon the Reserve near the Lake, and that they procure such road cut 16 feet wide and made passable for wagons and to be Completed by the first day of December next," a matter of only eight months. This was too much of a job for so short a time, and General Edward Paine, who cut it, got only as far as Westfield. "About all General Paine did," says the historian of Chautauqua County, "was to cut away fallen trees and underbrush and make the route over the firmest ground and the best places to cross streams. He built no bridges." The road was later completed to the Ohio line by settlers along the way.

As a matter of fact, the road was created as much by the wagons which struggled along it as by General Paine. By 1810 there were settlements at Cattaraugus, Silver Creek, Westfield, and Chautauqua Creek, but the road was bad as Hale discovered. For a man on horseback there was a better alternative—the road on the beach. Melish followed this road for most of the way from Grand River, east, but it was impossible for Hale and his wagon. Leaving the tavern at Buffalo Creek, Hale and Johnson

> started from the creek on to Lake Erie terrible traveling sand up to
> the horses fetterlocks in sand [,] rocks and stones in great abundance,
> and traveling 26 miles, which the people say was a very great day's
> journey. I finally made out to a house considerably from the road.
> Thunder & lightning and rain. I had to bait my horses until 9 o'clock
> and then tied them up by the head all night. I woke in the morning
> and the rain ran thro the Roof into my face bill 37 cents.

This house was probably just west of Angola and the bill seems about what it should have been.

The next morning Hale and Johnson "started again and went thro a most horrable road four miles and come to a creek," the Cattaraugus. "The wind blowing a gale and drove the water into creek with Logs and all kinds of trash but finally got into a boat, Drawed the wagon in by hand and so got over."

This ferry was owned by Captain John Mack and it was a "broad flat bottomed boat large enough to transport teams of all kinds," according to the Chautauqua historian. It was drawn across the stream by an ingeniously fastened rope, at least in normal weather. Captain Mack had a tavern, built of wood and two stories high, on the western shore of the Creek. Jonathan writes, "We staid two hours took breakfast, & had the best rum sling that I have drank since I came from home." Crossing the ferry, "breakfast, etc., cost me $1.00."

"I then went on as far as Holmes Tavern where I fared very well. Peck of corn, lodging, etc., etc. cost 81 cents. Traveled only 17 miles." If the roads were "horrable", the taverns along the Lake were good, in most cases at least. Holmes' was in the neighborhood of Fredonia and it happened to be the 4th of July, though Hale doesn't mention the fact or a suitable celebration.

The following day, however, Hale remembered to mention a family event of importance:

> This Day my Son William is four years old etc., I started from Mr. Holmeses and went on thro the woods where it is almost equal with the Beach Woods for roughness, & here I found a good Jack-knife with a 4/2 sticking in with the blade.

The little knife is now on display in the house Jonathan built in Bath, along with the compass he used on the trip and no doubt on the roads and in the woodlands of the Western Reserve. At Holmes' or perhaps along the road he "gave 25 cents for a peck of corn. Oats and corn is very scarce, and went as far as Widow Perry's Tavern where I fared very well."

Melish stopped at the widow's house too, coming inland from the beach to do so. He describes it as being near "Chatauque Creek", and Hale had trouble there. "I had a most horrable place to cross just before I got to her house," he wrote, "the Bridge was broken and I had to go round about 3/4 of a mile and a very sharp steep pitch. I carried away yoke to my Waggon just as I got to the bottom which providentially did no harm, etc." That day he traveled only 21 miles. The next day Hale and Johnson had another mishap which deserves to be told in Jonathan's own words:

> I set out from Mrs. Perry's and went on about four miles when I espied a large flock of pigeons. [Carrier pigeons, of course, which are now extinct.] I ask Mr. Johnson I had better see if I could kill a few he

answered he would like to see me kill a few accordingly I loaded my
Gun. I left my [horses] untied and then gave a shot which frightened
my Horses to such a degree that they started like a gallop and from a
gallop into a ful run, which soon upset my waggon. Cast both my
horses upon their Beam ends. When we both came up and unharn-
essed them. When they both got up unhurt to my surprise. I then
looked into my waggon where I see my chest lid split open all the
old trumpery was scattered over the ground. I picked up things as fast
as I could and set matters to rights, & upon examination I found my
whiffletree hooks was broke. I then put in my things and tied up my
waggon with ropes & went on about half a mile where I found a
Blacksmith who mended my waggon and then set my horses shoes
& here I took Breakfast which cost me $1.50.

Jonathan was lucky to find a blacksmith so near, but this proves again
that accommodations along these roads were more convenient than most people
today believe. This was because the settlements were slowly filling up, and
a blacksmith was essential to any community. The one Jonathan found may
have been in Ripley or someplace near it. But the travelers ran into trouble
again. They "went on about one mile when luck would have it that I must
run over a stub" or stump, "which broke one spoke and carried away one of
the Braces to my Waggon which I tied with ropes, and went on as far as
Moreheads, or Broadheads," he adds as a joke, "where my bill was $1.06 fare
none of the best neither." Because of the annoying interruptions, or in spite
of them, they traveled 19 miles that day and in spite of the stub, the road
was "pretty good too." By now they had passed into Pennsylvania, two or
three miles beyond Northeast.

*   *   *   *   *   *

When Jonathan awoke in the morning he "found a man from Middle-
town in Connecticut. I thought I would avail myself of the opportunity of
writing to my wife, accordingly I did, etc." A great deal of correspondence in
these years took advantage of such "opportunities"—the chance to send a letter
by someone going in the proper direction. This was usually far faster than the
mails. Unfortunately this letter alone of the four Jonathan sent back to Glastonbury during these months has not survived. From another letter, we know that
the bearer's name was Stow.

The two travelers "started from Moreheads and went on 10 miles [to]
what is cald Presqueisle," which is Erie, of course. One year later Melish
reported that it had about 400 people, a court house, jail, school, 76 houses
and three stores. "But", added Melish, "the place appears dull."

Jonathan and Mr. Johnson stopped at one of the three taverns Melish
reported, and got the "waggon mended again which cost me 50 cents & my

Breakfast & Bitters Cost me 50 cents more. I then went on 18 miles more thro some gulfs and Hollows & finally had to put up at a private house, where I got some hasty pudding and milk for supper the house being crowded with no less than four moving families." The place was so crowded, in fact, that Hale was "under the necessity of taking the soft side of a Barn floor for my Lodging. But however I slept very well. Horses fared poorly, my bill 50 cents good currency."

July 8th was another Sunday, but Jonathan traveled without apology, for he was growing anxious to reach his goal. He wrote humorously, "I started from the Barn floor and traveled on 5 or 6 miles thro a most terrible place and stopped at an old Dutchman's where I got some Breakfast." This was another private house. "There being no tavern, I had to do as I could, of course."

After breakfast, Jonathan wrote without the excitement one would expect, "I then took my horses and went on into New Connecticut, or into the bounds of it. Crossed what is called Conneought Creek and went on and put up at the sign of the Elkhorn where I fared pretty well." Melish, next year, crossed what he called the "Conneoght river" by a wooden bridge, close to the lake shore, and Hale probably did the same. The spelling of both these men makes more sense than "Conneaut." The Elkhorn was a tavern of course and it probably stood within the limits of the present city. Lodging and supper cost only 81 cents and Hale reported that he had traveled 21 miles, which proves the road was bad—or the breakfast and bitters at "Presqueisle" were long.

Monday morning Hale set out from the Elkhorn and went on for breakfast at Mr. Sweet's "on the banks of the Ashtabula, which we crossed [on] a pretty bad road." This was Peleg Sweet, a Rhode Islander, who was a tanner as well as a tavern keeper.

"I then went on," Hale continued, "as far as Harpersfield," actually Union-ville in the northwest corner of the township on South Ridge Road, "and put up at Judge Wheeler's where we fared very well supper Breakfast lodging horse keeping & Bitters cost me $1.12 cents."

This was a many-sided coincidence, though Jonathan and the Judge had no way of knowing it, as they chatted over their bitters in the room with the big fireplace called in Connecticut the "keeping room." As it happened, Judge Aaron Wheeler was married to Margaret Harper, the oldest of the eight children of Colonel Alexander Harper. One of her brothers was Captain James Harper, who with Abraham Tappan had surveyed the boundaries of Town-ship 3, Range 12 three years before. Tappan, in fact, was also James' brother-in-law, for he had married Elizabeth Harper. James and his crew, as we know, were quite likely the first white men to see Jonathan's land, barring a hunter or two.

But this is not all. The youngest of the Harper children was Robert. In 1815 he built a sturdy frame house about a mile down the road from Wheeler's, known today as Shandy Hall. It was inherited by the grandchildren of still another child, John Harper, and was given by them to the Western Reserve Historical Society as a museum. And to bring the story somehow full circle, in 1956 the house Jonathan himself built in the Valley also became a museum of the Historical Society in good part through the efforts of its late president, Laurence Harper Norton, one of the grandchildren of John.

One wonders which of these Harpers shared the supper and perhaps the bitters with Jonathan that night. The Judge and Margaret, of course, and possibly James and John, young Robert and the Tappans. The Harpers and Judge Wheeler were among the great landholders of the Reserve, owning shares in the Harpersfield Land Company which had bought six townships, three on each side of the Cuyahoga.

"Here", Jonathan went on in his diary that night, "Mr. Johnson left me. Here he took his box of goods which he put a board me at Buffalo after I had ship'd mine on board the boat for Cuyahagua," which was Jonathan's original spelling of the name until he finally reached the Valley. "I left at his Generosity to give me what he thought was right accordingly he gave $3.50, which was more," by twenty-five cents, "than I gave for the freight on my effects. His goods were not half as heavy as mine. Traveled 25 miles."

On Tuesday, July 9th, Hale, traveling alone once more, "started from Mr. Wheeler's and went thro the woods ten miles not a house to be seen." This was along South Ridge Road in Madison Township. At Grand River he probably crossed into Painesville by a bridge down in the valley at Main Street. He "bated" his horses here but did not mention the town by name, though Melish found in Painesville "a tavern, a store, and an excellent saw and grist mill, a fulling mill, and a wool carding machine." Hale then went on as far as "Esquire Murry's where I fared very well but poor horsekeeping. My bill was 69 cents. Traveled 22 miles." This would have taken him into Mentor.

Hale's remarks about Cleveland and its environs are tantalizingly scanty. It is interesting, though, that in these early years he always spelled the name "Cleveland", not with the "a" which the General added. In later years he adopted the "a", probably because it was used in the *Cleaveland Herald* until it was dropped from its masthead in 1832. However, both spellings were used by literate people like Elisha Whittlesey from the founding of the town.

Jonathan's diary gives the place brief notice: "I set out again thro some pretty rough roads, sharp pitches and logs." Melish too found bad roads west of Willoughby and the Chagrin. "I then arrived in Cleveland," Hale goes on referring first to the township, and he stopped at the "town at the mouth of the Cuyahagua where I put up at Mr. Miles here I fared very well, etc. Bill 83 cents. Traveled 27 miles," in spite of the pitches and logs.

This was probably Samuel Miles who kept a store at the corner of Superior Street and Seneca Street, now West 3rd. This is all Jonathan tells us about the place. According to Charles Whittlesey's history of early Cleveland, there were only 57 people living there in 1810 and it had not been incorporated as a village—though Melish reported sarcastically that it called itself a *city*. Its wood or log houses were scattered along West Superior, Water Street— now West 9th—and down the hill to the river on forgotten Union and Mandrake Lanes. A small wooden court house and jail stood in the northwest quadrant of Public Square, and beyond that was forest, broken by the track of Euclid Road.

But though the town was small and plagued with the "fever and ague," a disease we shall come to know better, even Melish had to admit that its location on the bluff was beautiful and important. The fact that it stood at the junction of the road along the Lake and the ancient highway south along the Cuyahoga, was the reason both Hale and Melish stopped at the place and that Abraham Tappan and Turhand Kirtland had made it their headquarters during the survey west of the river.

Hale must have stopped there, too, to pick up the luggage he had shipped from Buffalo but it apparently hadn't arrived. He had it "fetched" to him after he reached his land in the Valley.

On Thursday, July 12th, Hale wrote briefly that he started "from Mr. Miles and went on to Boston and put up at Mr. Bishop about 4 o'clock in the afternoon where I was very handsomely treated." As a settler and obviously a capable one he was naturally welcomed warmly. "Here I staid all night, it being 9 miles from the place where my land lies." One can imagine that Bishop and Hale talked far into the night.

That day Hale had traveled 21 miles, south along what is now Broadway across Kingsbury Run and on to Mill Creek and Newburgh, which was a larger and healthier settlement than Cleveland. At Bedford, where the next year Melish was to spend the night at another "small settlement", Hale crossed Tinker's Creek and headed down the Portage Road, which roughly followed the original Route 8 of modern times. Part of this road, in Boston Township, Melish declared was the worst he had seen yet in America. This seems hardly possible, for Hale said nothing at all and his time was fairly good. He turned off on the road to Boston, no doubt only a track from Hudson, and wound down the steep slopes into the Valley which was to be his home.

Bishop was Timothy Bishop, later a town judge. He apparently had the biggest house in the little community of some twenty or thirty people, for the following year a meeting was held there at which the Township of Boston was organized. The house stood on the east bank of the river.

The next day was Friday the Thirteenth, but bad omen or no, Hale left his wagon at Mr. Bishop's and "took one of my horses and went onto the ground thro the woods, a crooked narrow path of nine miles." This was the first time he mentioned a "path" on his journey west.

But he had reached his Promised Land. What he found there is part of the story of the settlement of the Valley, but the tale of his journey is not complete without mention of the trials of Theodore Hammond. This takes us back a bit.

On the 7th of June, 1810, Thomas Bull had written a letter to his agent, Turhand Kirtland, who lived in Poland, a town in the extreme south-eastern corner of the Reserve. The letter told Kirtland of the sale of 1600 acres of Bull's land in Township 3, Range 12 to Hammond and Hale. Un-fortunately he sent this letter by Theodore. In a postscript Bull remarked that if Theodore should need any help, his father Jason would be well able to pay Kirtland for it.

As it turned out, Kirtland's help was very much needed, and Jonathan's as well. For on July 11th, the day on which Jonathan's wagon reached Cleve-land, Theodore wrote a pathetic and almost illiterate letter to Kirtland from the town of Adamsburg, twenty five miles east of Pittsburgh on the Pennsylvania Road. This was some hundred miles west of Poland and shows again that this difficult mountain road was much slower than the route Jonathan chose. Theo-dore's letter, verbatim, is as follows:

> Mr. Turhand Kirtland, Esq.
>
> Sir i was directed by Mr. Thomas Bull to appy to you for Assistents if I got into trubble I have got as far as Addams burge and one of my oxon is taken laim And I cannot get a long and if you seand a Team to me by Chester Bishop who I have sent on and i will se yo sattesfied whin i got to your house
>
> Theodore Hammond

Assuming that Jonathan was already on his land, Kirtland sent him word of Theodore's "trubble" and also sent Bishop back to the east with another team. Jonathan wrote Mercy about what had happened:

> . . . I got here Eleven days before Theodore. He worried out his oxen. He sent Mr. Bishop almost a hundred miles to Judge Kirtlands for a yoke of cattle to help him on, & I hearing of this disastter I took one of my horses and went on to his assistance to Judge Kirtland where I met them all in good health.

However, this version ignores some other amusing facts Jonathan tells us in his diary. On Sunday, July 22nd, he wrote: "I arrived in Poland. I took one road & Theodore another but I overtook him about Sundown a joyful meeting indeed, etc. etc." This was the end of Theodore's comedy of errors and the two reached the Valley that Tuesday. It would seem that Theodore left Poland before his uncle arrived, or that Jonathan went on east to meet him.

Jonathan's diary ends with the note, "traveled 646 miles according to my journal." This must mean from Glastonbury to the Valley without the trip to Poland. If so, it is a remarkably accurate estimate of the mileage he covered, though perhaps a little short.

According to the notes in his diary Jonathan spent $27.26 on the way. But he forgot to mention a few of his expenses for lodging, breakfast, and horsekeeping, and for some reason be ignored all the tolls he must have paid. But the total could hardly have come to $50. While this seems small today for the 32 days on the road, in the currency of 1810 it was a large amount and of course it had to be paid in cash.

V

THE DIFFICULT MONTHS
July - November, 1810

Around noon on July 13, 1810, Jonathan drew up his horse in front of the cabin belonging to Aaron Miller which he had of course expected to find on his new land in the Valley. As it turned out, the cabin and the patch of clearing around it were not on Jonathan's land at all. They stood on Lot 10, overlooking Hale's land on the north. His arrival was no surprise, and Jonathan spent that night with the Miller family. "Very well treated but rather an unwelcome messenger," he wrote in his diary, for he believed that Miller was "expecting that I should oust him off his land." With his dry sense of humor he added, "Nothing to pay here." "It rained very hard in the night and some" in the morning. Unhappily, it turned out to be an unusually rainy summer.

During these first few days Jonathan was in for surprises, for Aaron was by no means the only squatter. In the middle of Jonathan's Lot 11, in the northeast corner of his land, was another log cabin with a sizable clearing already planted in wheat, the work of Captain Abraham Miller, probably Aaron's brother. Further south on the Hammond land, across what now is Ira Road, still another cabin had been built by a squatter named Gibson Gates. Someplace nearby, perhaps on the Hammond land to the south, there seems to have been shacks or cabins built by Aaron and Moses Decker, and there might have been one or two more. Historians of the township say that all these squatters arrived in the spring of 1810, but the year was most likely 1809. At least the Millers and Gates could hardly have built their cabins and cleared their land in the few good months they had in 1810. Furthermore, we know that Aaron made a trip back east, no doubt to pick up his wife and child, and that he may have left the Valley sometime in April.

Jonathan's diary goes on, "I then got help," from Aaron no doubt, "and went back after my waggon at Mr. Bishop's and got under way through the woods." He found it, of course, "a most horrable road where a waggon scarcely ever went before, and we got there just after sundown." He may have been the first to bring a wagon through. Back at Aaron's, he "treated them with some of my Old Antiga which they liked very well." This drink, which had been in the wagon all the way, was probably rum made in the British West Indies island of Antigua.

The next day was Sunday. "Here I be on the ground," Hale wrote that night. "Plenty of visiting, as much as 10 or 15 visitors, which was not very agreeable to my feelings." No doubt the Old Antiga flowed but this was not the way Jonathan preferred to spend the Sabbath. Some of the visitors may have come from the adjoining lots in Boston, for Jonathan had close relations with these settlers in the following months.

The final entries in Hale's diary give us a brief glimpse of his first experience with frontier life, and the frequent rains did not make them any easier. On Monday "I turned my horses free in the woods," which no skilled frontiersman would have done, "and today we looked all day for them and could not find them. I gave one dollar for looking," apparently to one of the Deckers, for the next day "Mr. Decker" found them. They were uninjured, "which very much eases my feelings."

After finding his horses, Jonathan "went to the mill in Northampton and got some flour, $1.69." This was the mill Aaron Norton had built in 1803 in the little valley where today Route 8 crosses Mud Creek. It was used by settlers as far away as Northfield, though it took them two days for the trip over the almost impassable road. Jonathan and Aaron did business together for years.

If Jonathan did not have rights to Aaron Miller's place on Lot 10, he certainly did to Captain Abraham's cabin and clearing on Lot 11. Legally, Jonathan could have evicted the Captain without compensation, but O. W. Hale, the grandson who wrote Jonathan's biography, tells us that instead his grandfather traded the Captain his horses and wagon for the valuable cabin and field. Jonathan had good reason to find this a bargain, for the wheat Miller had planted was a godsend and the clearing and cabin saved him months of backbreaking labor. He was able to use Theodore's oxen and wagon until Mercy arrived with another yoke, and in the inventory he compiled that fall he lists another horse. By making a deal like this with Miller, who seems to have been a man of some consequence and a veteran of the Revolution, he no doubt made friends in the Valley. He had probably found after a few days work at clearing his farm that oxen were vastly superior to horses in logging and in plowing his sodden unbroken land. There is no evidence, however, that he made a similar deal for improvements with anyone else.

While these negotiations were going on, Theodore made some sort of a deal with Gibson Gates for his cabin, and most likely a planted clearing too, on Lot 30. During the summer Theodore added to the size of this cabin, probably with a lean-to and an attic.

As for the squatters who had been dispossessed, Abraham moved just over the line into Boston Township and continued to be a prominent member of the community. Gates shows up in the 1820 Census as living in Northampton, probably along the river. In later years Jonathan had frequent business dealings with both these men. Aaron Miller seems to have stayed nearby for a few years at least, for he too had close relations with Jonathan and his family. But the Census for 1820 shows him living in Portage. What happened to the Deckers we do not know, but like many squatters with the frontier in their blood, they probably moved on west. The Millers and Gates had come to stay.

The day after he went to Norton's Mill, Jonathan wrote that "This day I felt very unwell, unable to sit up only part of the time. I expect it is the water, by drinking very freely." It was probably a touch of the fever and ague, but whatever it was the Old Antiga must have helped. It was probably at about this time that Jonathan moved into Captain Miller's cabin, or rather his own, for the day he recovered he writes that he felt much better and that "Captain Miller had a hog killed by the Bears which," the hog that is, "he brot home and drest which [was] terrably mangled." Bears and wolves haunted these early settlements for the next few years, feeding on hogs and sheep. Jonathan's invaluable diary ends with his trip to Poland, and his final entry was on Monday, July 23, 1810, after his return to his cabin.

* * * * * *

Before Mercy and the families left Glastonbury, Jonathan sent back home four letters full of advice, instructions and other matters. The one he wrote in Owego we have already quoted. He sent by a Mr. Stowe of Middlebury, Connecticut, a letter he wrote at Presque Isle, but either Mercy did not receive it or it has been lost.

The third and fourth letters have fortunately come down to us. They were written in Jonathan's cabin and are important documents on the early history of this part of the Western Reserve and of the problems involved in moving a family west. The first of these he dated July 30, 1810. It was certainly the first to bear the address "Hammondsburgh", at the top of the first page in Jonathan's hand. On the back of the letter he wrote mailing instructions for Mercy—"Direct to me, to the post office in Stowe, Portage County, State of Ohio." The postage was 25 cents, the usual price for mail from the Reserve to Connecticut at the time. As early as September 10, 1810, Jonathan's brother Jehiel used the address "Mr. Jonathan Hale, Hammondsburgh, Ohio", but the letter was brought along by Mercy and not put in the mail. Stowe remained the post office for the Hales until 1822, when one was established in what was by then the Township of Bath.

As we know, Rial McArthur, when he surveyed the township back in 1807, had informally called it "Wheatfield", and the name was used occasionally for years. The name "Hammondsburgh" was probably chosen in Glastonbury before Jonathan set out for the West. It was logical because Jason Hammond was older and more prosperous than Jonathan, had bought more land and had the first choice. The letter was postmarked August 3rd. This, and an equally important letter Jonathan wrote on August 14th, deserve to be quoted at length, with comment as we go along.

Hammondsburgh July 30, 1810

Dear Wife

    I arrived here on the 14th Inst much worn down and tired after a journey of thirty-two days. [Then comes the passage about his trip to Poland, quoted above.] It has rained almost three weeks here, & still continues to rain, which makes horrable traveling, beyond description. Wheatfields [on the Miller lot and elsewhere] all ready to harvest of excellent wheat all falling to the ground and some growing as it stands up. The land here is much better than I had expected [,] the farm that I shall have of one Hundred and fifty acres is full equall to our Onion Garden (except in a few places) & Mr. Hammonds is still better if possible.

This was very interesting news in Glastonbury, for the rich, black bottom land along the Connecticut River was the pride of the town and its farmers. But the reference to the farm of 150 acres is mystifying, for Jonathan had bought 500 acres from Bull. It probably refers to the prime land in the Valley which Jonathan planned at the moment to clear and plant. The rest he meant to leave in woodland or perhaps as pasture—and this is pretty much what eventually happened. He also sold 60 acres on the top of the hill to his brother-in-law Elijah Hale a few years later. He goes on:

    There is five or six families on this ground and [they] have made considerable improvements which I am under Obligation to pay [for] according to the Golden rule but according to Law they cannot get one Cent. I now live with Captain Abraham Miller in the house that is on my land, the best House that is in Hammondsburgh.

In this interesting passage Jonathan uses "ground" to mean his 500 acres. Captain Miller's seems to have been the only house on Jonathan's land, but squatters like the Deckers and Aaron Miller, and perhaps one more, may have cleared some of his excellent soil. If so, the only clearing which made a permanent mark in the family traditions was Abraham's "Miller Lot", which still bears the name. It lies to the south of the barn now used as a Pioneer Farm Museum.

    In his letter Jonathan then refers to his financial problems in Glastonbury and adds some helpful interesting advice for Mercy, Jehiel, and Jason Hammond:

    I hope that Mr. Welles has secured that Money to you in such a manner that my adversaries cannot get it, for I find that money to be a cash article here. I advise you to fetch no more heavy articles than you are obliged to, get two pair of shoes apiece [,] a side sole of leather (which is very scarce here I've given 25 cents for a pair of soles for my Boot) & get a set of Tea cups and stow in a tight box among your clothes and a few plates.

Mercy must have wondered about the tea cups and plates, which Jonathan forgot to explain, for she knew he had packed some in his wagon. He brought this up again further on. These and the following passages point out frankly the difference in the life Mercy would find on the Cuyahoga compared to that she would leave behind. What were every-day items in Glastonbury were not available at all in the Reserve.

> Get that cloth at Mr. Cromwells and what cloths our folks can spare. Not many sheep here [,] scarce any flax to be had here, perhaps you had better join with Mr. Hammond and get a Box of Tea or part of a box, and a cask of gunpowder. For good powder we can get [a price] almost double what it cost there. Get my old Boots footed or fetch some upper Leather etc. and a great many other things that I cannot think of now perhaps you may think of.

Undoubtedly one of the reasons Jonathan came on ahead was to plant some crops to feed the family over the winter. Captain Miller had spared him some of the labor by planting winter wheat the year before, but Jonathan reports:

> I'm now about sowing my turnips but it is so wet we cannot work half the time. I forgot to mention that I broke most all the plates & likewise most all of the Tea cups & Saucers, pitchers [two illegible words] and two glasses etc.

This breakage may well have occurred along the Lake the day he shot the pigeons and scattered his "trumpery" when his horses ran away.

> I've wrote two letters before now, one when I was at Owego and one when I was at Presque Isle by Mr. Stow which I expect you have received. I wish you to write me as soon as possible for I want to hear from you & from my little Children & still more to see them. You may depend that I had but a small Idea what I had to undergo when I set out. I can tell you that the Journey is very great, be careful of your health, drink not too much water, drink spirits freely & be sure to give it to the children. I repeat it again be very careful with yourselves.

Jonathan advised the Glastonbury party to follow a different route than the one he had traveled, probably because of the unfinished pike and the hated Beech Woods in Pennsylvania. He suggested that they come by the town of Hudson on that river, then north to Albany and west by way of the Albany Turnpike. But after talking to other travelers, it seems, he revised this plan in his next letter.

> I would advise you to take the Northern road, to Hudson which [?] etc. go on to Buffaloe and put your heavy things on board a vessel and come on the shores of Lake Erie which is terrible bad traveling, on that account I advise you to go light etc. etc. I [have] many things to write about but I have not room. Give my best love & respects to my Beloved Mother, for her good counsel and advise & likewise to my loving Sisters. & likewise to Mr. Hawes a beloved friend of mine. I ask the prayers of you all, for my health, prosperity, and may Heaven's richest Blessing ever attend you all which is the prayer of your true and ever loving Friend and Effectionate Husband

> Jon^a Hale

Mrs. Mercy Hale, Glastonbury

That summer the rains continued and fevers swept the cabins in the Valley. But on his farm Jonathan made progress with his clearing and planting, and the jobs in and around the cabin. It seems certain that Jonathan did all this work himself, with occasional help from Theodore which he returned in kind when a job required it. Hired help was out of the question in these months and the account book we will turn to later, mentions none. No one had time to do it and Jonathan had nothing to use for cash or barter. The last of the four letters Jonathan wrote to Mercy deals with this difficult and critical summer:

Hammondsburgh August 14 1810

Dear Wife

This is my fourth letter ["third" is crossed out] that I have wrote you since I left home, one dated June 29 and one in July about the 8th or 9th [the missing letter] and the last one was dated 30th stating my safe arrival, my success, of my Land, etc. which you have undoubtedly received. You will recollect that I could not think of all that I wanted to write. I wish you to get pay of Col. John Hale for two or three Barrels at a reduced [price] if you can't get no more, sell all other affairs or things that belonged to me (except Mother wants them) & appropriate to where I owe. I likewise forgot to mention to you to pay Mr. Dickinson which I hope you have payed. I hope you got some money by fishing to pay here & there for your necessities, if you have no money ask Mr. Wells for some which I dare say, he will supply you with some.

Write me the appearances & Prospects of things in old Glastonbury and about the farming business, Grain, Garden & Grass and what success you had in your harvest gathering. I hope Mr. Dart has been as good as his word respecting helping you [,] give my respects to him, tell him I live in an Onion Garden.

This homely little joke was meant for Abiel Dart who was the Hale's handy man about the house, garden, and farm in Glastonbury in 1809 and 1810. The account book shows that Dart cleaned wells, worked on fences, and did just plain "work". Jonathan must have yearned to have him around in the wilds of the Reserve with so fearfully many chores to be done. Since his last letter, more memoranda had occurred to him:

Purchase such articles as you want for yourself in wareing apparel, such things are scarce here, get some Pepper & spice some Drugs & medicines, Essence of pepper mint, [illegible words], Opium which is good in fever & Ague. Get a Copper Kettle and get a Plow share for there is no plowshares here a few pounds of nails to nail up my Tables & Doors & a great many other things that we shall want to eat and Drink.

Nails were a critical item and hard to come by in the Valley for the next few years. Jonathan procured many of those he needed in later years by barter, usually from men in Tallmadge, but in 1810, it seems, even this was impossible. Jonathan continues:

> The season has been uncommonly rainy here which makes it very unhealthy. Especially the fever & ague, there is one half the people here shaking over fever & ague. I cannot say that I enjoy a very good health, but I hope when the weather becomes clear and the ground dry it will be more healthy. [Two words illegible or erased] we have sowed about an Acre and a half of Turnips & mostly cleared up five acres of Wheat Land etc. etc.

> The best way for you to come, to take Lenox Turnpike to Albany from there to Skenectady & then on to Utica & then to Canandaigue, & then to Buffaloe & put your things on Board a vessel, and come on the shores of Lake Erie.

The problems concerning this route is to trace the "Lenox turnpike to Albany", which he mentions as though it were well known—and there was plenty of gossip about these roads all over the Western Reserve. Lenox is a lovely old town in the mountains of Western Massachusetts a few miles from the New York State line, but it has no good, direct access to the West. It is more likely that the road Jonathan had heard about followed his own to Litchfield, then northwest to Canaan on the Housatonic, Sheffield and Great Barrington in Massachusetts, and northwest into New York State, by-passing both Stockbridge and Lenox. Such a road appears on maps of the early 19th century but there is no evidence that it was a turnpike. From Albany on, the route followed the great road along the Mohawk as Jonathan had written. On his own trip he had reached it near Geneva. He ends his letter with a sensible suggestion, based on his knowledge of the "horrable" Lake Shore trails and on his hunger to see his wife and children:

> Send us word if you can when you get to Buffaloe we will come with oxen and horses to help you. I'll try to write again before you set out if I can. Give my compliments and love to Mother, Brother, & sisters & all that inquire after me, Mr. Lockwood and family.
> Adieu J. Hale
> To my Beloved Wife, Mercy Hale
> Glastonbury

*   *   *   *   *   *

Just as important as clearing and planting, Jonathan knew from bitter experience, was a better road through the Valley. He needed far easier access to Boston down the river and the road which climbed the hill to Hudson, and also up the river to the Portage and the gateway there to the growing settlements at Stow and Tallmadge and to Norton's mill. The Hales and Hammonds would need supplies from these places and eventually they would provide the farms with markets. And with the families soon to come with three wagons heavy with supplies and household goods, there was no time to lose.

During the rainy July and August, Jonathan talked with his neighbors about cutting a road, and with men like Timothy Bishop and the young surveyor Alfred Wolcott, who also lived in Boston and later taught school. Jonathan was the leader beyond any doubt. On August 28th he went to Ravenna, the seat of Portage County in which Hammondsburgh lay, and asked the Commissioners for permission to cut a road, offering to pay the costs.

The Commissioners' minutes read:

> Jonathan Hale presented a petition signed by Timothy Bishop and others praying for a road beginning at Pontey's Camp on Columbia Road thence on the most eligible ground to the Cuyahoga Portage near Joshua Kings, and said Jonathan having given bond to pay the costs, Abraham Miller, Andrew Johnson, and Alfred Wolcott were appointed a committee and Alfred Wolcott surveyor to view said route.

Pontey's Camp was the old, probably abandoned Indian settlement on the river at Boston. Columbia Road, such as it was, led from Hudson through Boston into Richfield Township, which at the time was called Columbia. "The most eligible ground" from Hale's point of view naturally led through his land. An early historian, W. A. Goodspeed, says that this road was the first to "touch" Bath Township. To do this the road probably followed the one called River View Road today, turned west at the crossing now known as Everett to follow the present Oak Hill Road past the Hales, then back to River Road at Botzum. General Bierce in his history says Hale paid $5 for the "privilege" of cutting this road, but the County Commissioners paid the cost of the survey. On December 26, 1810, they "gave Alfred Wolcott award of sixteen dollars and 10 cents for his services as Surveyor, the Committee Chairman, and axmen's services on a road from Pontey's Camp to Cuyahoga Portage."

The axmen were naturally local people—Jonathan may have been one of them—and the path they cleared for Wolcott's chains may have served as a track which slowly grew from daily use into something like a road. Jonathan may have stood the cost, which would certainly have been more than $5, of improving the track during the fall and winter, for the date given for the road by the township historians is 1811. At least the road was in better shape than Jonathan had found it by the time the Hales and Hammonds arrived.

As we have seen, the migration of the families was a joint affair, one that required careful planning. Jonathan and Theodore had gone ahead to explore the ground. Jonathan's letters to Mercy were reassuring in regard to the farmland and the location, and the squatters' cabins and clearing were good news too. But he had told the Glastonbury people that the journey was hard and that in the Valley they would lack almost all the things which helped to make their homes so comfortable in Connecticut. Life would be primitive, until by their own hard work they made it something better.

The summer and early fall were busy for the women in the three households. In addition to her other chores, Mercy had to spend a good deal of time doing whatever she could to wind up Jonathan's complicated and rather unhappy financial affairs. Almost all of the furnishings in Jonathan's mother's house, where he and his family had been living, were left behind because they belonged to her. Rachel and her two unmarried daughters, Ruth and Abigail, would live alone. Mercy had been warned to travel light, and she seems to have brought such things as food, kitchen tools and utensils, and clothes, as well as replacements for the cups and dishes Jonathan broke on the way. Some of these were packed in chests which came in handy in the cabin. It is doubtful that she brought any furniture of importance for none has survived, and there would have been no room, Jonathan hinted, in the wagon. And the cabin no doubt was already "furnished", with crude home-made tables, benches, and beds.

According to the Hammond genealogy, the party left Glastonbury on September 28, 1810. Mercy and her three small children and the household goods filled a wagon drawn by a team of oxen. Sophronia was six, William four, and Pamelia, whose name was always spelled this way, was only two, the youngest of the party. Jonathan's sister Sarah and her husband-and-cousin Elijah Hale had another yoke of oxen and two more children—ten-year-old Eveline and six-year-old Mary. The Hammonds had a team of horses, and their family records say that Jason's oldest daughter Rachel, "then a young woman of nineteen years, drove the span the entire distance of about 650 miles." It is likely that Jason drove Mercy's yoke of oxen. The three other Hammond children were old enough to be of help; Lewis was sixteen, Mary fourteen, and Horatio twelve. The Hammond genealogist says that "Jason's nephew, Elijah Hammond, of Bolton, accompanied them as far as Cleveland, where he turned back home." Many another weary traveler westward bound turned back before he reached his destination.

Thus there were eight Hales and seven Hammonds in the little caravan, though only six Hammonds arrived in the Valley. Which of the two routes suggested by Jonathan the families followed to reach the Hudson we do not know, but there can be no doubt they came by way of Albany, Utica, and Geneva and from there traveled the same route Jonathan did, for Elijah Hammond turned back in Cleveland.

Such journeys as these fascinated the people who remained at home, and they reacted in a variety of ways to the adventure and the problems involved. One reaction was that of Jonathan's older brother Jehiel, a merchant who traveled up and down the Atlantic coast and was also a wit. The two brothers were on the best of terms and in their conversation and correspondence Jonathan had been "Old Kelley" and Jehiel "Old Doyle". In a letter he sent west with Mercy, "Old Doyle" wrote that in his latest travels he had "got himself a wife in Kennebec". This turned out to be an Indian squaw. But more important, like thousands of other Connecticut men, Jehiel had a burning interest in the Western Reserve. He wanted to know "what soil water and climate" Jonathan found there, and "what your prospects are and how your family got on and what kind of government and Religion you have in your State. What kind of game and fish and what is the produce of your country and what timber (,) insects, etc." The reason for all this was that Jehiel, a restless sort of man, was thinking of moving West. However, he died in Glastonbury eight years after he wrote this letter. Jonathan's careful reply to Jehiel and the similar inquiry made by Joseph Wright, we will turn to shortly.

As an appendix, so to speak, to Elihel's genial and interesting letter is a mournful note written by a pious and fearful neighbor, Clarissa Caswell, which shows a very different view of the western migration. She wrote:

> I suppose I must say something I hardly know what but one thing
> I will inform you is that my very heart aches for your poor Wife and
> family. I did not tell her so. I hope it is all for the best that she
> is going on this journey but how she is to get there with the load
> is beyond my comprehension, but I wis[h] some of you to write me
> how they get there if they ever do.

They did get there, and it is just as well that Mercy brought this discouraging postscript with her. The trip took about six weeks compared to 32 days for Jonathan's. The families did not travel at all on the Sabbath, the oxen plodded slowly along, and the loads in the wagon were heavy. We know no details of their journey, but toward the end of October as the Ohio Indian summer faded, the weather and the roads must have grown worse.

Jonathan did not go to meet them, as he had suggested, for on September 28th he was stricken by a violent attack of the "fever and ague". Nor could Theodore have gone because he had to dress and undress his uncle and no doubt helped him in other ways. But the families made it alone, breaking their difficult way along the track the surveyors had cleared in the Valley, reaching the cabins in the first week in November.

The Hammond records say the travelers arrived on November 5th, and if so the trip lasted 42 days. But Jonathan made his first Hammondsburgh entry in his old account book on November 4th, and it seems likely that Mercy had brought it with her. Jonathan had had need of the book, as his entries show, for he obviously predated several items to October without giving the day. Some weeks later Jonathan wrote that the trip of the three families took seven weeks, but this is clearly a lapse of memory.

Captain Miller and his family had of course moved on and Jonathan was living alone, or with Theodore for company, when Mercy and the children arrived. Mercy not only received an affectionate welcome from Jonathan but he had very great need for her care. She and the three children transformed the drab little cabin, and from that time until the death of Jonathan's grandson in 1938, the home of the Hales, whatever it was, was bursting with life.

* * * * * *

Jonathan recovered slowly, and on November 26th he was finally able to answer the requests he had received from both "Old Doyle" and his nephew, Joseph Wright, for information about the Cuyahoga country. It is certainly the most interesting and historically important of all the letters Jonathan wrote, even though only a few of them are known today. He describes in simple, observant detail the farm he lived on and the country around it. We have very few such descriptions of these pioneer farms. Perhaps more important, he tells us what a migrant from Connecticut could accomplish on a farm in the wilderness in the space of less than five months. And Jonathan's poor health and the abominable weather pretty much cancelled out the advantage he had received from taking over Miller's cabin and clearing. Then, Jonathan Hale undoubtedly brought to the Western Reserve a higher intelligence and greater skill than the average settler from Connecticut. When he was well he could also work like a horse, for like all the Hales he was a big man, more than six feet tall, with a large-boned craggy sort of face.

The letter we have which is addressed to Jehiel is a copy made in Jonathan's hand of the original he sent by way of the post office in Stow. The first half of it deals with matters other than the farm, but they have interest too, especially the rather salty relations with his brother.

Hammondsburgh Nov 16 1810

Dear Sir

I received your letter by the hand of my Wife 7 weeks from the time she started from home and to my surprise found that Old Doyle had returned from a cruise richly laden as I understand with nonsence and squaws, with many other articles of a combustible nature to tedius to mention!!!

But Sir I congratulate [you] on your safe arrival on the American shores, wishing you all the success in Discharging your cargo & Seamen (as well as nonsence), and your cargo disposed of as quick as possible, and your Pockets filled with true Wisdom and Integrity that you may enjoy all the good things that you have toiled so hard for, and finally upset your adversary [a man named Brainard with whom Elihel and Jonathan were both engaged in legal quarrels] in the ditch of dispair   Amen.

You write [that the] Brainard cause come to trial last week, that it proved to be a foolish trial that the Court are ashamed of their proceedings. I think it is high time they were. They had better look [back] a few sessions and see what eronious Judgments they Established.

After this amusing piece of foolishness, Jonathan goes on to the more serious and important part of his letter; opening with a report on his health:

> You wish me on the receipt of your letter to write you a particular account of this Country. Sickness has prevented my complying with your request, ever since the 28 of September but one week since my ague left me. For a number of weeks my Nephew had the task to dress and undress [me] for the greatest part of the time should you see me in a strange Country you would scarcely know me, the Bulk that I used to form is rendered a mere wreck of bones, in comparison to my former Robustness. I refer you [to] Mr. Joseph Wrights letter which 'tis likely he will show you [in regard to legal matters].

> I live about ¾ of a mile from the River Cuyahogua which empties into Lake Erie at Cleveland [sic] about thirty miles from where I live. The land I live on is as good as any man can wish for. This country abounds in various kinds of timber (Viz) white oak ash hickory Black Wallnut sugar maple which grow to a great size 5 & 6 feet in diameter cherry boxwood butternut Beach whitewood and cucumber tree which bears a substance resembling a cucumber most excellent to bitter whiskey etc. The land here what is called the Reserve what has fallen under my observation is Generally uneven but nothing so much so as old Connecticut. The woods abound in various kinds of herbs such as spikenard Balm of Gilead Mint snakeroot Gensing and a great many more that I cannot think of now.

> And wild animals a plenty such as Deers Bears wolves which make a terrible howling some nights enough to tear the earth up, Raccoon, plenty black Squirrel millions of them, not many beavers, Otters & Muskrats in abundance Turkeys plenty ducks & I'm told there is Geese in the spring in the Rivers and ponds. Please to let Mr. Joseph Wright see this letter for he requested me to give him description of animals which I'd forgotten to do in the letter untill the letter was full. The climate here is considerable different from old Connecticut altho in the same latitude. The last Winter the people tell me that cattle and young horses did very well by cutting a few maples once in a while etc.

It seems to have been the people who did the cutting, not the animals! The following brief and important paragraph tells us about the state of the farm after the season was over in 1810:

> I've got in five acres of wheat which looks very well I've bought [?] two acres of corn I've one horse & one cow two hogs that would weigh 60 apiece, as nice ones as ever you saw and half [?] of a fat one. We have 1 pair of fat oxen one however we have just butchered which weighed about one thousand. I've about eighteen acres of land under improvement pretty well fenced thirteen acres of which would produce if well tended 70 Bushels of corn pr acre.

I understand that you was rather affronted because I took some few of your things. You have ever told my [me to?] take & use untill you called for them I wish Brother Wright & you would settle and let my wife have what things she has got which put at the highest price would not amount to more than $40.00.

I wish you to write me when convenient especially if you have any news. Give my love & respects to my beloved Mother tell her that I have thought of her noursing arm [?] in my sickness. Give my love & respects to my sisters & all enquiring friends

Your Friend and Brother

Jon^a Hale

Copy of a letter to Jehiel Hale

Jonathan's account book adds to what we know about his first six months on the land in the Valley. His entries concern in good part two men we already know—Abraham Miller and Aaron Norton. It was from Miller, who moved to Boston after leaving Jonathan's land—buying the land, we can assume, instead of squatting—that he bought the two hogs he lists in his letter. The price was $2 each. He bought two "fowls" from Miller for 12½ cents each which add something essential to his inventory which he did not mention in his letter. He also bought three bushels of potatoes. And Abraham, surprisingly, was credited for mending shoes, though Jonathan supplied "a piece of soal leather" worth 34 cents. In January, 1811, Jonathan also supplied Abraham, to balance his account, with a half-pound of the powder Mercy had probably brought, a jack-knife— not the one he found on William's birthday, for that we still have— a pair of horseshoes, "a couple of boards", two bushels of wheat, and two quarts of whiskey.

This was the simplest kind of barter, with the shoe repairing the only unexpected item. Being a squatter for a good many years, Abraham must have learned how to make simple repairs in order to have something to put on his feet.

Jonathan's account with Aaron Norton, the Northampton miller, is also pure barter, though he had had to pay cash for his purchase of flour. On November 4th Norton bought what may have been the exhausted yoke of oxen Mercy had driven from Connecticut, though when he wrote to Elihel, Jonathan still had a yoke. This interesting account with Norton reads: "To Yoke of Cattle to be paid in good merchantable wheat and whiskey by the 4th of Jan. 1811 amounting to fifty three dollars." Oddly, on the credit side of this deal there are entered only 6½ bushels of wheat, 2 gallons of whiskey, and 2 bushels of corn, which by no means balanced the account.

The most interesting of these meager accounts for the last months of 1810 is one with Joseph James, dated in December. We know nothing about James save that he made barrels and similar wooden containers. In the days before cans, such containers were essential to life in the cabin and on the farm. Jonathan bought from James two "provision barrels" for $1.05 a piece. These were for the storage of flour and similar dry products and there is a barrel in the basement of Jonathan's house in Bath today which may be one of those he bought from James. He also bought a swill pail for a quarter, a tub which Mercy probably used for washing, for $1.25, and a whiskey barrel for a dollar.

Due to the system of sale and settlement used by the Connecticut Land Company, most of the Reserve in these early years was a heavily-forested countryside sprinkled with an occasional isolated farm. Travelers often wrote about breaking through the wilderness to find well-planted fields surrounding a single house and its outbuildings. But the families in the Valley were luckier. It is obvious that a little farming community—though not a village by any means—existed as early as 1810 in the northeast corner of Hammondsburgh and the adjoining parts of Boston and Northampton Townships. The rich "onion garden" of the Valley was what drew these settlers to the area, that and perhaps the sense of protection from wandering Indians they found in the sheltering hills.

VI
SETTLING THE VALLEY
1811 - 1825

The log cabins the Hales and the Hammonds lived in during their first years in the Valley were typical of those in the rest of the Western Reserve. For one thing, they were crowded with adults, children, and babies, with dogs and chickens that wandered in, and an occasional Indian begging for whiskey. Mercy brought three children when she came from Connecticut—Sophronia, William, and Pamelia. On December 11, 1811, Andrew was born, and he acquired fame in the Valley as the first child born to settlers, ignoring the squatters, in what is now Bath Township. On November 19, 1813, a baby girl named Abigail was born and lived a brief ten days. Mercy's last child and her fifth surviving one was James Madison Hale, born on June 4, 1815. Thus two adults and five growing children lived in the cabin for most of the sixteen or seventeen years it was used as a house.

Down the road, six Hammonds and four Elijah Hales lived for about three years in a cabin which was probably smaller than Jonathan's. Theodore had built an addition, perhaps a lean-to, but it could not have been much help. The crowding was due to Elijah's financial troubles back home, but in 1813 Jason and Jonathan helped him acquire land on the hill. Jason and Sophronia, "for the love and affection they bore them," gave Elijah and Sarah fifty acres they had bought from Thomas Bull in Lot 14. It lay along what is now Ira Road, and a frame house Elijah built in the thirties still stands on the site. Jonathan sold Elijah for $200, no doubt on credit, sixty acres of his own land in Lot 14. They were back from the road toward the ravine of Hale Run and it was there that Elijah built his cabin.

Many years later Elijah's granddaughter, Eveline Bosworth Cook, in the engaging memoirs we shall mention often again, described this cabin in which she lived from babyhood until she was ten years old.

> . . . the fireplace was on the east side of the room . . . a ladder in the southeast corner, chests under it, than a south door of two rough boards nailed together with cross pieces top and bottom, with wooden hinges and [a] latch with string, which was "always out", a small window beside it, then Aunt's [Mary Hale's] loom and other things in southwest corner, no window in the west but a cupboard, grandmother's bed in the northwest corner . . . next was a window, table and cupboard and north door next the fireplace, and front of that was a plank that could be taken up, and underneath was all the cellar they

had, was perhaps 3 to 4 feet deep, with a barrel of pork on the side and bin for potatoes on the other. . .

The house had "one room below and chamber", meaning a loft to which the ladder led, and "sometimes in the morning would see snow in places on the floor, but would go between them barefoot to the ladder." For years they used a "noon mark" on the sill of the south door instead of a clock.

Jonathan's cabin must have been much the same. We have an imaginative but not very accurate lithograph of its exterior, outbuildings, and the farm land around it made from a drawing by Albert Ruger. He was born in Germany and married a daughter of O. W. Hale. The drawing is based on the recollections of James Hale, the youngest of Mercy's children, who lived in the house until he was ten or eleven years old. Ruger made the drawing around 1880 when James was 65, and at about the same time he also made a drawing of the present brick house and its grounds. For contrast, both drawings are reproduced on pages 78 and 79.

The earlier drawing, which concerns us here, shows smoke pouring from a chimney on the east end of the cabin. On the other end is a lean-to with a door, and part of this may have served for the pigs that ran in the adjoining pen and the rest for the storage of tools or "provisions", like flour and salt which had to be kept dry. The window must have been on the rear. There was space for a "chamber" or attic, and certainly a need for one with five children crowding the house. It is interesting to recall that this cabin was "the best House that is in Hammondsburgh".

Mercy is carrying a pail toward a small log building which covered a cellar, an improvement on Elijah's more primitive arrangements. It was used for pork, apples, turnips and other produce which needed cold storage. There is a shallow depression in the grounds of the present Hale House which marks the site of this cellar. Chickens are pecking away in the yard and Jonathan is chopping a log. Another small cabin with a chimney, standing near the road, was used as a tool house and shop and according to tradition served for a couple of years as a school. The larger barn, back from the bend in the road, was for cattle as well as the wagon which stands in the passageway. One side, or an attic, may have been used for hay. West of the cabin is the pig pen and in front of it a row of six beehives.

Toward the hills, the land is still being cleared—undoubtedly an anachronism in relation to some of the other improvements—and cattle are grazing among the stumps. There is no sign of the crops Jonathan reported to his brother, but the Miller Lot, which was sowed in wheat, lies outside the picture to the left. In the road are a yoke of oxen, and a wagon that might have been used for hay or the rails for the fences which line the road and wander off into the fields. Near the barn a horse is dragging along the road a barrel in one of the few conveyances known to the Indians.

Across the road is a clay pit we shall hear much more of later, and near it are three neat piles of brick. There is no sign of a kiln, which is something we would like to see. In the foreground at the left is a group of story-book Indians which clearly appealed to Ruger—a tepee, squaws, braves, and all the rest. There had been Indians on the top of the ridge behind this scene, but they had certainly vanished in the days of the cabin.

In the right background is another cabin which is undoubtedly Aaron Miller's, but it should be two or three hundred yards to the north on Lot 10. An amusing detail is the double maple which grows at the end of the line of trees at the extreme left of the drawing. It also appears in the second of Ruger's drawings. Mr. Carl Cranz, who farmed the place in the days of C. O. Hale, also remembers it. It is one of the curiosities a boy would recall and it was probably flourishing in James's childhood. On the hillsides above the Valley there are still enormous maples which we know were growing in the time of the Indians.

Ruger shows an apple orchard, newly-planted behind the pig pen. One can doubt James Hale's accuracy here, for the site has been usually used for crops or meadow and Carl Cranz remembers an old family tradition that Jonathan's first apple orchard was on the ridge across the road, overlooking the river.

*   *   *   *   *   *

When the laggard spring came to the Valley in 1811, the Hales and Hammonds had survived their most critical winter, and as spring moved into summer the life in the cabins and fields was hard, but it was full of hope. Quite suddenly, that fall, a dark fear swept over the Valley and the townships east of the river. For the first time in the brief history of the Western Reserve it was threatened with a raid by the Indian tribes from the Maumee Valley, with all the horrors that would bring. To the settlers on the west bank of the Cuyahoga the threat was immediate.

There had always been Indians around the Cuyahoga settlements, remnants of the Ottawas and Mingoes who had once lived in this hunting ground and then moved West. The ones who remained were a shiftless lot, looking for handouts of food and whiskey, stealing hogs, chickens, and corn, and sometimes offering game and furs for sale. Mercy Hale is said to have treated them kindly, more so than her neighbors believed they deserved. But no one thought of them as a menace.

The Indians who threatened the Valley in the fall of 1811 were something else. Encouraged by the British in Canada, the great Indian leader Tecumseh

Air view of the house and farm looking toward the northwest. About 1945.

Ruger's reconstruction of the Hale cabin and its surroundings.

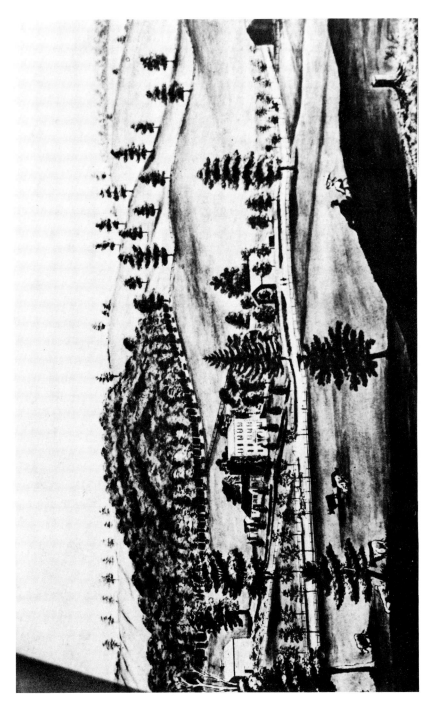

For contrast, Ruger's contemporary view from the same site. They date from about 1880.

The house Jonathan built in the Valley, as it looked in the '80s and '90s.

Jonathan was born in this Glastonbury house and lived there until migrating West.

The old sugar house in its Victorian prime, around 1900.

A summer-time view of the farm, across the Valley to the western hills.

A glass plate made of the house showing the north wing.

A glass plate of the house showing the south wing. Both plates were made the same day and before the wings were bricked.

83

after my Waggon at Mr Bishops and got under way thro the woods a most horrable road where a waggon scravely ever went before, but we got there just after sundown here I treated them with some of my Old Antiga which they liked very well &c &c

---

Sunday July 15th 1810 Here I be on the ground here so plenty of visiting as much as 10 or 15 visitors which was not very agreeable to my feelings &c &c

Monday July 16th 1810 I turned my Horses into the wood yesterday to day we looked all day for them I & and could not find them I gave one Dollar for looking it rained very hard most part of the Day &c &c

Tuesday July 17th 1810 I went again aft my Horses, where I track of them & Mr Decker found not one off, which very much eased my feelings. this day went to the mill at N. hampton & got some bloomeal $1.69

From Jonathan's diary, a page describing his arrival in the Valley in 1810.

84

*Daguerreotype of Sarah Cozad Mather Hale and Jonathan,
probably dating after 1845.*

*Four of Andrew's children, Clarissa, Pamelia, Sophronia, and C. O.
A daguerreotype of about 1854.*

Whitcraft's general store at Hammonds Corners.

*Vacationers arriving at Ira Station on the B&O
for a stay at Hale Inn.*

*Andrew Hale's sheep and cattle barn,
now the Pioneer Farm Museum.*

The Western Reserve in 1829, drawn by a student. The counties have long since been divided.

88

was arousing the tribes in the Maumee Valley to regain the hunting grounds they had lost at Greenville and Fort Industry. The Cuyahoga country was filled with rumors which suddenly became a fact. A large force of Indians appeared in arms on a bluff above the Portage. Its chief was known as Onandaga George.

"The Indians were sulky," General Bierce writes, "and Captain George, as he was called, would flourish his tomahawk and scalping Knife in apparent defiance." The site of the camp was chosen well, for the bluff above the Cuyahoga where it turns to the East is a key to the eastern townships of the Reserve. The war party was waiting for word from Tecumseh and its signal fires burned through the night.

What precautions the settlers took in this frightening emergency we do not know, but after a day or so of tension the Indians suddenly vanished, their camp fires still smoking on the bluff. Three days later the people of the Valley and of threatened towns like Hudson, Stow, and Tallmadge, learned the thrilling news of the victory of William Henry Harrison over Tecumseh at Tippecanoe. Onandaga George had learned of the battle by runners or signals, and he and his men had fled in panic.

Though this was the last real threat the Indians made to the country along the Cuyahoga, tension rose again the following year. The quarrel with England over the freedom of the seas did not particularly interest the settlers west of the mountains. But they were vitally concerned, especially in Ohio and Kentucky, with the traditional British alliance with the Indians in the western country. In this great forest land, war with the British meant war with the Indians.

The United States declared war on Britain on June 18, 1812. The War Department ordered General William Hull to advance to Detroit with a small force of volunteers, including some from Southern Ohio and the Western Reserve. He was to occupy the fort at Detroit, cross the river to Canada, drive the British from Malden, and march into Western Ontario. But he was old and cautious and Washington had failed to send him supplies. When he reached Detroit he was surrounded by Indians and a handful of their British allies. What happened has been a matter of debate ever since, but it is doubtful that Hull, with his supplies running out, had any choice. On August 15th he surrendered his entire force and the fort at Detroit, leaving the Ohio settlements exposed to the British and, what was worse, to the Indians.

The terrifying news was brought to Cleveland a few days later, when a handful of canoes full of Ohio volunteers paroled by the British crept into the river mouth. They were wrapped in blankets and the settlers took them at first for Indians. Their fearful tidings raced up the Cuyahoga and for the next two months the Hales and the Hammonds kept their rifles ready, their eyes wandering to the dark line of the forest as they did their chores, their cabins dark, and the doors bolted at night.

Governor Meigs of Ohio at once called out the Militia, which in theory, at least, meant every man who could carry a gun, and General Elijah Wadsworth at Warren was put in command of the four feeble divisions to be raised in the Western Reserve and the counties to the south. News of the war reached the Valley by rumor, and more reliably in the little weekly paper with the wonderful name of *The Trump of Fame,* the first in the Reserve and published at Warren. We know it was read in Boston and it must have reached the Hales and Hammonds too.

Early in September *The Trump of Fame* wrote that Wadsworth's "headquarters are in Cleveland, 36 miles from the Huron River, to which place Brigadier General (Simon) Perkins has marched with 500 men for the purpose of building blockhouses to guard the frontier settlements." This crucial but feeble line of defense stretched south to Mansfield, and word reached the Cuyahoga settlers that the Indians had raided as far east as Norwalk, killing and burning. But by the middle of September, 2,000 Kentucky volunteers were on their way up the Miami Valley and this was comforting news. In its issue of September 23rd, *The Trump* reported other good news, closer at hand:

> General Wadsworth, we are told, has removed his headquarters from Cleveland to the Portage between the Cuyahoga and the Tuskarawas branch of the Muskingham, after having sent reinforcements to General Perkins at Huron. The object of this movement, we are told, is to open a more direct communication between Pittsburgh and Sandusky, and to facilitate the transportation of canon and artillary stores to the Michigan Territory.

To accomplish this, Wadsworth began to cut a road from the Portage to General Perkins' stockade at Avery, near Milan on the Huron River. It apparently left the Valley by the route to Smith Road. This activity so near at hand brought security to the settlers along the river, but it also brought the calling-up of their men into the 4th Division of the Militia, covering Portage and Cuyahoga Counties.

For safety's sake, the Hales moved all their women and children into Jason Hammond's house. "As they were packing up," O. W. Hale records of Jonathan's family, "among other things they took the brass kettle, and filling it full of the more valuable articles of kitchen furniture, dug a hole in the chip yard and buried it. Their son William, a lad of six years, seeing that the pudding stick had been overlooked, took it and carefully hiding it under a splinter of rail, it was safely kept until peace was restored, when it was brought forth . . . and served to stir many a dish."

It is a family tradition that Jason and Jonathan were called for the Militia, but there is no reason to believe that Theodore and Elijah were spared, for the story relates that no one was left at home but the women to protect the children and cabins. When the men, whoever they were, appeared at Wadsworth's camp, pitched in a field at the Portage under the bluff where Onandaga George had burned his signal fires, they asked to be excused from service because they were obviously needed at home. Wadsworth agreed—though perhaps only for Jason and Jonathan—but on the way home they ran into the General's son who thought they were deserters and brought them back to camp. The General sent them home again.

By the middle of October, Wadsworth moved his men westward along the road to Huron and the worst of the danger was over for the Valley, though it was not until General Harrison marched his Kentucky and Ohio men to the Maumee that the Reserve could feel truly safe. And the brilliant victory of Commodore Perry near Pelee Island in Lake Erie on September 10, 1813, ended the danger forever.

*   *   *   *   *   *

The threats of Indian attack in 1811 and 1813 slowed down the settlement of the Valley and the townships to the east. But in the summer and fall of 1813, a new trickle of migration began. The Census of 1820, however, scarcely records a boom. It gave the township, then called Bath, a population of 176 persons in 33 families, but a few people in the more remote areas were probably missed in this early count. Among the newcomers was Calvin Hammond, Jason's prosperous brother who came from Boston in 1815 and gave his name to Hammond's Corners, at Ira and Brecksville Roads. Another was Dr. Henry Hudson, the township's first physician who also taught singing and lectured on religion. He and his son Thomas settled near Bath Center. There were a number of millers doing business along the rapids and falls of Yellow Creek, and in Ghent there was a chairmaker and a blacksmith. The remaining settlers were farmers scattered widely across the township.

The upland part of the township, mostly a forested plain, was remote in these early years from the narrow strip of the Valley, and the Hales had closer ties with the people of adjoining townships who lived near the Cuyahoga. Boston had 275 people and 48 families in its river bottoms, runs, and gulls, and Jonathan did business with a good many of them. There seems to have been a scattering of farms near the hamlet that was first called Unionville and is now known as Everett, about a mile from Jonathan's cabin. The Iddings family settled there, the Beers, Abraham Miller, and Abner Robinson, the local poet and wit we shall hear more of again. Northampton had a population of 287 and Richfield 315. Even Hudson could boast of only 491 white settlers and 8 Indians. These figures, of course, are for townships five miles square.

As we know, Township 3, Range 12 had been called Wheatfield by Rial MacArthur and was known informally as Hammondsburgh after 1810. But the township had not been organized, and to take this step a meeting was called in what is now Bath Center in 1818. According to the not-always-reliable General Bierce, the subject of a name came up and there was considerable sentiment for making Hammondsburgh official. But Jonathan Hale, "who had something of the wag in him, replied 'Call it Jerusalem, or Jericho, or Bath—anything but Hammondsburgh.'" It was promptly voted to call the township Bath.

This story, on two counts, has a very unlikely sound. Jonathan's relations with the Hammonds, as far as we know, were as cordial in 1818 as they had been in 1810 when he was the first to use the name Hammondsburgh. And why did he suggest the unlikely name of Bath? He had no family ties with the town in England that we know of, nor did the Hammonds. There is no Bath in Connecticut or Massachusetts, favorite sources for place names in the Western Reserve. And it is hard to see why Hale or anyone else at the meeting should have chosen the name of a fashionable English watering place for the quiet township on the banks of the Cuyahoga.

The reason for the choice of a name is lost in local myth, and we do not even know the names of the township's first officials. There is a story that Dr. Hudson was named the first Justice of the Peace, and if it is true the choice was good.

*   *   *   *   *   *

Jonathan's account books are important sources for our knowledge of the steady progress he made in developing his farm. They also throw light on the life and economy of the neighborhood he lived in during the years between 1810 and 1825. Within this period the account books show that the Hales and their neighbors began life in the Valley dependent almost entirely on the things they brought from the East, and on what they could grow in their clearings or hunt and fish in the forest. From this simple beginning they created a far more complex economy, and that is our story here.

The account book Jonathan began to keep back in 1804 and Mercy brought with her to the Valley, is by far the best authority for Jonathan's farm. Very briefly, it tells the story of his almost total dependence on barter in the earliest years, and the gradual increase in the amount of what he always called "cash"—coin or printed money. His first entries, as we saw in 1810, are almost solely records of barter. This continued during the trying time of the War of 1812, but as the years run on the accounts became increasingly records of payments made in cash or in credit that was based on cash.

Whatever accounts Jonathan kept after 1825 have not been preserved, but we do have a little book which Andrew used when he was running the farm between 1844 and 1850. As we shall see in a later chapter, barter was still in use but most of Andrew's accounts were settled for cash. Still later, Andrew's son, C. O. Hale, kept accounts and no barter was involved at all.

Jonathan's brief accounts for 1811, the year of Tecumseh and the alarm at the Portage, still show a far more limited range of entries than those for the last few years he was living in comparative comfort in his ancestral home in Glastonbury. The only hired hands he lists are his cousin Elijah Hale and Henry Iddings of the Boston family. They reaped for a total of 4½ days at $1.00 a day. The only work Jonathan paid for that might be called skilled was "stuffing" a saddle, for which he credited William Beer, another Boston man, 25 cents on two occasions. Jonathan also exchanged 6½ gallons of whiskey and a small piece of "soal leather" for a young sow and a pair of geese.

There is one strange entry in 1811 which will concern us later in more detail. It reads: "To my violin, price agreed $7.00." Was it the pressing need for cash that forced Jonathan to dispose of a thing so precious as his violin?

Between the Battle of Fallen Timbers and the declaration of war on England, things were quiet again in the Valley. In the spring and early summer of 1812, Jonathan hired his friend Gibson Gates, now living along the river in Northampton, for eight days of threshing, plowing, and "dragging logs." This is almost the only reference we have to the clearing of land which was still going on. The bulk of this back-breaking labor Jonathan must have done himself. Gates was especially useful, for he brought along a team of oxen for which Jonathan also paid. For this work and other items Jonathan exchanged three crops which he had not mentioned before in his accounts or letters. One was 11½ bushels of potatoes to various men at 40 cents a bushel. In 1810 he was buying potatoes from Aaron Miller. The others were 5 pounds of tobacco at 20 cents a pound, and a bushel of oats which he traded to Gates for 45 cents. The potatoes and oats we would naturally expect, but the tobacco was rare for the Reserve and he may have brought the seed along from Connecticut or had it sent. He traded tobacco for the next few years and then the entries stop. It is interesting too that in his "onion garden" he grew no onions worth a mention in his book of accounts. The reason for this was the fact that onions grown in quantity, as he grew them in Connecticut, required a quantity market and none existed in the Cuyahoga country. In the spring of 1812 Hale also exchanged for other items one "fowle", 4½ pounds of flour at 3 cents a pound, and a small amount of leather.

On the credit side of the little book, early in 1812 Jonathan obtained 7 gallons of whiskey in exchange for potatoes. At about the same time Benjamin Dane, still another Boston Township man, made a pair of shoes for Jonathan, another for six-year-old William, and "footed" an old pair for Jonathan. Though Abraham Miller had done amateur patching of shoes two years before, Dane appears to be the first professional cobbler in the Valley. His wife Dolly also did spinning for Mercy, and this is odd, for there were certainly spinning wheels in the Hammond house, if not in Jonathan's. All this work by the Danes was lumped together at a value of $2.25, balanced by edible items like potatoes.

That summer the renewed threat of attack by Indians, or even the British after Hull's surrender of Detroit, is reflected in Jonathan's account books. His entries dwindle away to almost nothing in August and September. The war brought a further scarcity of cash and what we would call today a depression, which lasted on into 1814, and this too reflected in the accounts. In these two years Jonathan records that he obtained a shoat from Benajah Dane in exchange for a bushel of rye, a grain he had not mentioned before, and half a bushel of corn. Henry Iddings spent three days reaping oats and hoeing corn and for part of this work Jonathan actually paid him in "cashe", the first such payment he lists for work of this kind since his arrival in the Valley.

These meager accounts are quite certainly not the total sum of Jonathan's transactions during these interesting years. A casual exchange of a "fowle" for a bushel of potatoes when he passed Aaron Miller's place with his wagon, might not appear in the book. But Jonathan was a careful man, as we know, and most of this sort of thing must have been written down. His account book leaves no doubt that his farm was close to being self-supporting. There was a good reason for this: He was forced by the pinched economy of the western country during these difficult years to make do with things he could grow or contrive to make, or obtain on a very small scale from barter. Yet the account books show that the farm was supplying each year, thanks to Jonathan's efforts, a slowly increasing variety of grain and other things. It is certain too that improvements in the cabin and the outbuildings around it made life more comfortable in 1814 than it had been in the fall and winter of 1810.

We have ample evidence that the economy of the Valley began to improve in 1815 and 1816. Cash began to flow, there was an increasing tide of immigrants, and far more goods were available to families like the Hales. However, barter remained a factor in all of Jonathan's account books, and it persisted for many years. It was a convenient form of credit, and money has never been an abundant commodity on American farms.

For instance, in 1815 Henry Point of Boston began to make shoes for the family. He made them for Pamelia, William, and Andrew in exchange for potatoes, tallow, flax, "part of hay stack", a bushel of wheat, and 14 pounds of salt. Tallow was made from the fat of pigs or oxen, flax and hay he had never sold before, and salt he must have been buying in quantity. All this shows that times on the farm were changing.

And for 1816 we have a most interesting account which is not in Jonathan's book. He received it from Jonathan Starr who probably lived in Copley and from all the evidence we have was a traveling peddler. There is no record of his owning a store in any of the townships of the Valley. The account shows that the range of goods available to the Hales and Hammonds had greatly increased since they arrived six years before, and that Starr depended largely on sales-for-cash.

The list of things Jonathan bought from Starr in 1816 and early 1817 includes some interesting items Mercy needed for her family sewing, and perhaps for the tailoring she had begun to do for the Valley people, as we shall see. These include "2¾ (yards) Blue Fuller Cloth", which was finished woolen cloth, probably not homespun. As we have seen, John Melish found a fulling mill and a wool carding machine in Painesville in 1811. Mercy paid "2 37½/100 per yd" for this, a total of $6.53, which seems like an enormous price for the times and the Hales. The cloth was probably made into pantaloons, a jacket, and perhaps a coat for Jonathan. Mercy also spent seven yards for callico at 50 cents a yard to make a dress for herself. Other items she bought were three-quarters of a yard of "sattenett" for $1.87½, perhaps for trimming the dress, cotton shirtings, "satten twist", and a paper of pins which cost her a quarter.

For the first time tea appears in the accounts when Jonathan bought a half-a-pound for what seems the enormous price of $1.50. He also bought a handsaw for $3.75 and a file to go with it for 31¼ cents, a supply of nails, and a knife.

It is clear that by 1816 the crudities of frontier life were vanishing, but that thanks to the "horrable" roads and the distant sources of supply for most of these items, prices for the times were high. Jonathan paid for some of these items with butter and eggs which Starr may have sold to his other customers. The account came to $35.00, and $13.26 of this was charged to men in debt to Jonathan. There was a quarter described as "Cash Not Current Money", probably scrip. But Jonathan did not pay the full amount on time and Starr charged him a dollar in interest!

In 1818 the account books list "1 sturgeon 1.00" and "1.25 paid for crockery in Canton." Clearly both the menu and the horizons were broadening. We also have an interesting entry which proves that Jonathan was improving his buildings. In the Ruger drawing, based on James's recollections, all the roofs are hand-hewed timber. But in 1818 Jonathan paid "Rice & Skinner" 75 cents for one day spent in shingling the barn roof. One can guess that the roof of the cabin was shingled before the barn's, and it is probable that Jonathan made the shingles himself. In the Pioneer Farm Museum now on the site there is equipment like that he used, and it may very well be his.

It is not surprising that Mercy's shears and needle were welcome in the Valley and filled a greater need than they had in Connecticut. But remembering the back-breaking work the cabin and the children demanded of her, it is amazing that she had any time free for "cutting and making". One important reason for doing the work was that she was often paid in cash.

In Glastonbury she had usually made the entire garment—a coat, a jacket, or a pair of pantaloons. In the Valley about half of her jobs involved the cutting only. Perhaps she could not spare the time for "making", but it is more likely that the families who ordered the work saved money by doing the sewing at home. Again, there is no evidence from her charges that Mercy supplied the cloth. It was spun and woven at home or bought from peddlers like Jonathan Starr.

As they appear in two of Jonathan's account books, Mercy's prices in the early years were about the same as they had been in Connecticut, running from $1.75 for cutting and sewing a great coat, down to $1.12½ for smaller garments. By 1820, however, she had added 25 cents to each of these prices. For cutting alone the price seems low—usually 25 cents no matter what the article was. Some of these garments she made are included in the lists of items used for barter, others were clearly paid for with cash.

Mercy's first customer, outside the family, of course, was none other than Aaron Miller. In April, 1811, she made a great coat for Mrs. Miller for $1.25, one of the few garments for ladies listed in the accounts. That fall Aaron placed an order which, by Mercy's description at least, seems like an unusual one for a former squatter. It was a "sourtout", and together with a "jacet" for his son it cost $3. Mercy must have been in the habit of making "sourtouts" for her clients in Connecticut. In Paris the *surtout,* or "coverall", was a long, close-fitting overcoat, quite elegant in fact. It is amusing that the name should turn up in the Valley for what may well have been a big, warm, homespun overcoat, fine for driving a yoke of oxen on a windy, snowy day. It must have served the purpose, whatever it was, for three years later Captain Abraham Miller bought another "sourtout".

All of Mercy's customers we can place from the local records lived in the southern part of Boston, and along the river in Bath, Northampton, and Copley. They included neighbors like Henry and Jonathan Iddings, Jacob Morter, and William and John Beer, all of Boston, Abel Vallin of what is now called Botzum in Northampton, and Moses Latta who had a mill on Yellow Creek. For a wedding in the Northampton Woodward family she made a "wedding coat" for the bridegroom for $2.50, the most she ever charged in these accounts, two pairs of pantaloons for $1.00 each and two jackets for $1.50.

This enterprise of Mercy's was a neighborhood one. A much more ambitious enterprise which Jonathan was engaged in for a number of years beginning in 1819 took him far beyond the limits of the Valley, to Hudson, Stow, and Tallmadge. He developed, in fact, what could be called the first new "industry" in Bath, other than the old standbys like milling. It was devoted to the burning and selling of lime.

In a growing community like the Valley, lime was becoming an essential product and was hard to come by. As log cabins and shacks gave way to houses built of saw-mill lumber, and brick and stone began to be used for basements and chimneys, there was a need for mortar. Lime is also the oldest chemical fertilizer known to man. But in virgin country fertilizers were an expense most farmers did not bother with or could not afford. We know of only one other lime-burning operation nearby and that was in Canton, an inconvenient distance for the customers who bought Hale's product.

The old "lime field" where the burning was done is easily spotted today. It lies on land sloping down to Hale Run in its upper reaches, on the north side of the little stream in Lot 12. The land is still clear of larger trees, but covered with underbrush and the remains of an apple orchard which was planted much later. The lime Hale burned was a fossil deposit found in rocks and boulders washed down by the brooks which feed Hale Run, or lying exposed in the fields and woods. General Bierce believed there is a large deposit of rock of this kind underlying the Run, but if so, Jonathan did not dig for it. He burned the supply that was easily at hand, and as he used it up, the burning petered out. These forgotten upland clearings are quiet places today, but in the years between 1819 and 1826, perhaps for longer, they were busy in the off-times of the year, when Hale and his boys had time to gather the stones and tend the fires, which had to be fed for at least twenty-four hours.

As Jonathan practiced it, no doubt by methods he had seen or even used in Connecticut, the job was simple enough. For the large-scale operations at the time, kilns were built of brick or stone, but there is no evidence or tradition that Hale used anything as elaborate as this. Instead he probably arranged the limebearing stone in a pile and over it built a "rick" of logs and brush, which he burned and fed for the required time. When the fire had cooled, the lime was sifted out from the debris of stone and ashes. It was packed in casks or bushel baskets and hauled down the long, rough path to the Valley. Though the burning was a seasonal operation, Hale sold his lime all year long, storing it in one of his small log buildings near the road.

For his sales of lime Jonathan bought a new account book in which he listed items between 1819 and 1825. It also contained entries for Mercy's needlework and some of his usual accounts for the barter and purchase of food and the like. Most of the lime was sold in casks, though the first year or so he sold a good many bushels. The word "cask" is a generic term and it is difficult to estimate how much one held. But during 1819 Hale lists a number of sales in a container called a "tierce", and they were made at the same price as his sales in casks. A tierce was normally used for wine and held 42 gallons. It was larger than a barrel, which held 21½ gallons of wine, and smaller than a hogshead which held 65 gallons or more. From the prices Hale charged for lime in bushels and casks, it seems that a cask held around six or eight bushels. He made no record of buying the casks, and he may have made them himself, from staves he had cut from his own timber in one of the new Yellow Creek sawmills.

Hale's prices for lime varied somewhat over the years he was active in the little enterprise. In 1819, the first year covered by his special account book, they range from $2.00 a cask to $3.50, with an average of about $3.00. At the same time he was charging 37½¢ and 50¢ a bushel. In 1820 his prices were usually $3.50 a cask, but he sold some for cash at $3.00. On one trip he made to Hudson that year he sold a cask for only $2.00, probably to get rid of it before he drove back home. During the next two years the normal price was $3.00 with an occasional sale at $3.50, and 50¢ for a bushel—though sales by the bushel dwindled away. Now and again he sold a "small cask" at $2.00 or "low quality" lime at the same price. From 1823 on through 1825 his sales fell to almost nothing, though they must have revived in the next two years thanks to the brick house and the Ohio Canal. We have no records for any of this lime.

Jonathan's sales of lime added up to a figure that seems unimpressive today but was worth many times more in those years. More important for Hale, most of his sales were for cash, or cash-on-credit. In the table below his sales are listed by years and are taken of course from his little account book:

1819	27 casks	63	bushels	$174.06
	13 tierces			
1820	77 casks	6	bushels	283.50
1821	66 casks	39½	bushels	228.45½
1822	71 casks	4	bushels	190.50
1823	7 casks	11	bushels	35.55
1824	4 casks	10	bushels	15.87½
1825		4	bushels	.75
	252 casks	137½	busheis	$928.69
	13 tierces			

Jonathan made a few interesting sales in exchange for goods, which are included in the table above. Tallmadge and Stow, it seems, had access to iron, either raw or in the form of nails, and Hale exchanged lime for these critical items on several occasions. A Mr. Jerrold of Tallmadge got seven casks of lime—the most Hale sold at one time to one individual—in exchange for iron, and Jonathan made smaller deals for two casks each with Dudley Griswold and Capt. James Neale of that place. Unfortunately, the account book does not mention the amount of iron involved.

We have an interesting letter Hale received from Captain Israel Thorndike of Stow. While it does not speak very well of Hale's business methods, it shows how such matters were handled:

> Captain I. A. Thorndike to Jonathan Hale
> Thorndike [part of Stow] August 22, 1821
> Sir:
>
> This is the third letter I have wrote you concerning some Lime. In consequence of what you seemed anxious for last winter, viz: that I should take some Lime of you for Nails; I concluded I would not purchase my Lime in Canton but have of you—I wrote you to ascertain if you had the Lime but as I have had no answer I ventured to send [for] the Lime and I wish you would write me by the bearer whether I shall send the Nails when I go after the second load—the Lime I think you informed me I should have for $2.00 per bbl. or 2.50. I cannot be positive—I shall want about 6-bbls—and I trust you will send me none but good. I write by the bearer.   Yours truly
>
> I. A. Thorndike

This was a bargain price, probably because Hale needed the nails. His account book shows on the following day, August 23rd, that the deal went through:

> Capt. Israel Thorndike
> To three Casks Lime   7.50
> To three do. do.   7.50
>   paid in nails

Obviously Thorndike's wagon could hold only three casks at a time, and when he made the trip in person to pick up the second load, he brought along the nails. Hale made a similar deal with Martin Camp of Tallmadge at the rate of $3.50 a cask, and he charged the higher rate because he granted credit. The sale was made in November, 1821, and Camp delivered the nails the following June.

Late in 1821 Hale sold two casks of lime to Nathaniel Oviatt, an important land owner in Richfield, at the high price of $4.00 a cask to be paid in wheat. The following year he exchanged three casks with Normand Baldwin, who probably lived in Hudson, for only $2.50 a cask to be "paid in goods or glass," and from this it sounds as though Baldwin kept a store. A Mr. Tyler of Copley also paid for a cask half in cash and half in salt. However, the large amount of currency Jonathan was paid compared to the goods he received in barter proves again that the economy was expanding.

Hale sold his lime to men living as far north as Aurora, Brecksville, and Mantua, and as far south as Coventry. Farther south than this it was probably easier to buy in Canton. But the great bulk of his sales were in Tallmadge, Hudson, Northampton, Portage, Stow, and Bath in that order. He sold to 99 individuals, and 21, more than one-fifth, were Tallmadge men. His great market lay in the older townships east of the river, for he sold to only 15 men who lived west of it, and almost half of them were his neighbors in Bath.

In most cases it seems that his customers drove their wagons to Hale's place in the valley to pick up their lime, though he sometimes sent it by men going in the right direction, or charged a dollar or so for making delivery himself. And as we have seen, he made at least one trip to Hudson on his own.

The lime business brought to Hale's door some of the most prominent of the men who were building the Western Reserve. Perhaps his most interesting customer was Owen Brown, the father of John Brown, who bought 3 casks on two occasions. But David Hudson, founder of the town bearing his name, bought nine casks, Judge William Wetmore of Stow bought eight on different trips, and he also sold to Aaron Miller, by then living prosperously in Portage.

In Bath, Hale sold to Dr. Hudson and his son Thomas, and also to Moses Latta who may well have used the lime to build his mill on Yellow Creek. In Hudson his distinguished customers included the Rev. William Handford, George Kilbourn, and Marvin Oviatt, as well as Owen Brown and David and Milo Hudson. In Northampton another old friend, Gibson Gates, bought lime and so did Judge Hezekiah King, who had a well-known house near Portage. In Stow, Timothy Starr and Captain Israel Thorndike's brother Edward, who owned a good part of the township, were customers. Hale also sold to other distinguished Tallmadge men, Asaph Whittlesey of a famous family, and Elizur Wright who became a trustee of Western Reserve College. And he had what amounted to wholesale dealings with one Anson Ashley of Tallmadge, who picked up lime in Bath on several occasions and delivered it to customers in his home town along the way, charging for the service.

But in 1822 another and even more interesting item appears in Jonathan's record of sales, and this was brick. As his account book shows, he and his father had made brick back home in Glastonbury. Soil permitting, it was only natural that he should make it in Ohio. He found suitable clay across the road from the cabin and a little south of Hale Run. On April 11, 1822, the first entry concerning brick appears in the account book he used for lime and the purchaser is interesting too:

Gibson Gates Dr	
1 cask lime	2.00
1200 brick 50¢ ctw	6.00
10 tile	.50

Twelve-hundred bricks would have built a chimney, or the foundation of a small frame house.

The next year Hale sold 300 bricks and other items to Judge Wetmore of Stow. In 1824 he sold 1404 bricks and a quantity of lime to Elisha Mather, or Mathers as it was sometimes spelled, apparently for use in a house he built near the Boston-Northfield line. The last entry is for 1825, when Jonathan sold 750 more bricks to a Mr. Parsons of Boston.

These were by no means the last bricks made by Jonathan Hale. In 1825 the idea was taking shape in his mind to build a house of brick for himself and his family. For this reason and because of the Ohio Canal he continued to burn lime on the hillside above the Valley. All this will be dealt with in later chapters.

* * * * * *

For Jonathan life in the Valley was not all hard work on the farm, in the lime field or in the clay bed. He still found time, on the Sabbath usually, for music. We know about this from several sources, and one is his nephew Joseph Wright, in passages he crowded into letters he wrote to his Uncle relating to news from home and Jonathan's financial affairs. They tell an interesting story. The first is dated August 7, 1817:

> I understand from your letters & from other sources that you have paid some attention to the business of instruction in musick. I think this must be tolerable employment for the winter if you can get good wages, not to say as high as Roberts has 60 dollars the month. You know we used to take great delight on the subject of musick & were it not for the trouble etc. I should send you something in this way which might probably divert a vacant hour.

Joseph assumes here that Jonathan is being paid for the teaching he does, and in a letter he wrote three years later he brings up the subject again, in a very literary, round-about way. "It seems that you are the principal teacher of Musick in that region. I did not anticipate when you left G. that you would be able to make your musical talents subservient to your advantage."

Later on in this letter Joseph adds: "I should be really happy to sing a few pieces with you, such as I have in my possession. The tunes now in vogue in Con. are of a very different description from those we sung when you were here. In G. the singing is very respectable. Plummer & myself have been the principal support of it since you left."

Soon after this, Joseph's interest in secular or social music waned, and in a letter he wrote in 1825 he makes no bones about it. After thanking Jonathan for a map of Ohio twenty-one-year-old Sophronia had drawn, colored and sent to him, Joseph goes on: "The tune you also sent me I also received & thought highly of it. But I acknowledge that I have nothing to do with it"—music, that is— "except sing on the Sabbath." Naturally, the subject of music does not appear again in the correspondence between uncle and nephew.

Though we learn a good deal about Jonathan's interest in music from Joseph's letters, his assumption that Jonathan was being paid for teaching music in these early years of the Valley is hard to believe, at least in regard to the churches. When Joseph reports that Mr. Roberts was making $60 a month, he apparently refers to a "wage" from the Congregational Church in Glastonbury for instructing and leading the choir. But in the Western Reserve, as late as 1839, the preacher himself in the church in Bath was paid only $200 a year and firewood, on a three-quarter basis. That teachers of music were paid at all is most unlikely.

But Joseph may have thought that Jonathan was doing private teaching, for he suggested that it could be done in the winter. What sort of a market there was for lessons in voice or the violin in the cabins, farm houses, and hamlets of the Reserve in the snow-bound winters around 1820, is anyone's guess. Joseph's notions, of course, were based on the rather cultivated world of Glastonbury and he had only a hazy idea of what life was like in New Connecticut. What Jonathan was doing beyond any doubt was teaching the music of the church to the young people of the Valley and its neighboring townships. He was doing it only because of his love for music and his deep religious feeling.

But Joseph does make clear that Jonathan continued to sing, play, and compose the sort of secular music he had loved in Connecticut. Joseph says he received a tune from Jonathan as late as 1825, and there is no reason to believe that this was his last. His violin and his voice became famous in the Valley, and his family loved them. One thing is certain, if he sold his violin for $7 in 1811, he certainly bought another as soon as possible. He taught Andrew to play the violin and both Andrew and William taught choirs in Bath. Elijah Hale's granddaughter, Eveline Bosworth Cook, remembered that in the 'thirties Jonathan used to play his violin at family parties and Andrew played the "clarionett." They used to have "such beautiful music", she goes on, such pieces as *Bonaparte's Retreat from Moscow*—surely a feat on these two instruments—*Boston March,* and *Hail Columbia.* "Oh, it was splendid", she adds. By then the music stores in Cleveland were selling scores for popular pieces like these arranged for almost anything.

But Jonathan appears in the histories of the Valley townships as the first teacher of the choirs in the struggling little churches—in Hudson, Stow, Tallmadge, and undoubtedly other townships across the river. While we know that he and his father and brothers sang in the Glastonbury church, we have no evidence that Jonathan ever taught there or any place else in Connecticut. But he inherited a sound tradition, and in the Western Reserve he found good use for it.

We have the hymn book dated 1791 which Jonathan's brother Jehiel gave him, and also the one he inherited from his brother Samuel around 1798. The brown covers are battered and worn from years of wear and on Jehiel's book Mercy's needle has sewn the torn pieces together with linen thread which still does the job. These were probably Jonathan's personal hymn books, and they were extremely useful in the elementary teaching he did, for both had instructions for singing as well as rich mines of old Congregational hymns.

Jehiel's book is especially designed as a handbook for "learners". Its title is typically elaborate for the age:

Select Harmony
Containing the Necessary
Rules of Psalmody Together with a Collection
of approved Psalm Tunes, Hymns and Anthems
By Oliver Brownson

The instructions this fascinating little book contains "In Forming and Tuning the Voice" are typical of the rest:

> Great care should be taken to avoid sounding through the nose, or blowing the breath through the teeth. High notes should be sounded soft but not faint, and by low notes should be sounded full but not harsh; notes should be struck and ended soft, gently swelling the middle of each sound, unless contradicted by the mark of distinction.

The instructions also contain "The Gamut, or Scale of Music", descriptions of the musical signs, and a few pages of "Explanations". The hymns and anthems are scored for four voices, and sometimes the words are written for a single voice in parts of the hymn. There are 83 hymns and other church pieces and most of them bear the names of New England towns. The last name of the composer is also given. Among them are such titles as *Yarmouth* by Benham, *Framingham* by Billings, *Norwich* by Hibbard, and a dozen or so by Oliver Brownson himself. But there is also a hymn of thanks called *Washington* and others named for Philadelphia, Virginia, and Georgia.

Most of these hymns have four brief lines to a verse. They were clearly written by amateurs, and one called *Worthington*, by a poet named Strong, gives a notion of how poor they can be:

Thee we adore, eternal name
And humbly own to thee
How feeble is our mortal frame
What dying worms are we.

But *Billings' Philadelphia* is a better example of the usual quality:

Let Diff'ring nations join
To celebrate thy fame
And all the World, O Lord combine
To praise thy glorious Name.

The second book Jonathan brought along to the Valley is not really a hymn book at all. It is more modest in scope and was "Designed for the use of worshipping Assemblies and Singing Societies" by Elijah Griswold and Thomas Skinner. It is in the same dilapidated shape as Brownson's book, or worse, but did not need Mercy's stitching. Its title is long but it was probably known by the initial words, "Connecticut Harmony." It contains psalm tunes, anthems, and "favorite pieces, many of which were never before Published". To this is added a condensed version of the rules and explanations found in Brownson's book.

The book was originally printed with only 26 hymns, but following these is about equal space which is ruled in staves but contains no words or music. In these empty staves some 25 hymns and songs have been added, some in a skillful hand that looks very much like type. One or two at the back are probably in Jonathan's hand.

While these books are important and deserve more study than they can be given here, we also have some charming material written in Jonathan's hand which gives us more authentic samples of the music Jonathan actually taught in the Cuyahoga country. One of these pieces is a tiny hymnal he probably held in the palm of his hand while singing or teaching. It has twelve pages, brown and fragile now, each eight inches wide and only three inches high. It is dated January 12, 1819, and Jonathan ruled the staves himself and copied on them the score and words for four of his favorite hymns, and the music alone for a fifth.

Some of the words are now illegible, but none of the hymns appears in Jonathan's other books. One of them can be read, a hymn named "Hope". It was written for children and its two verses show more charm and talent than almost anything he brought from Connecticut. They read:

> Come children, learn to fear the Lord
> And let your days be long.
> Let not a false or spiteful word
> Be found upon your tongue.

> Depart from mischief, practice love
> Pursue the ways of peace.
> So shall the Lord your ways approve
> And set your soul at peace.

The other hymns are named "Irish", or "Hymn 72, Book 2, Doctor Coates"; "Hartford"; "Psalm 8, with music by Mr. Bull of Hartford"—no doubt a relation of the Bulls we already know in a quite different way—and "Hymn 2, or *Springfield,* by J. Lloyd." For all these hymns, except "Hope", and for those in the other two books, only one verse is given, but in the front of the books from Glastonbury are printed as many as five verses for some of the hymns they include. Perhaps it was assumed that the singers knew all these additional verses and that in most cases there was no need to reprint them. The hymnals were primarily musical scores.

There are two other small scraps of musical material written in Jonathan's hand. One of them is a torn page listing the keys in which about twenty hymns—most of their names illegible—were to be sung. The other is a list of the "metres", or rhythmical structure, for what seem to be the same hymns. Some of the meters are marked "particular", some "common", and others are "long".

How Jonathan accompanied his students and choirs we do not know for certain, but we know that Andrew Hale, his son, had nothing more than a tuning fork when he led the choir in Bath in the 1830s. A violin would have been out of place in a church, at least, and organs must have been exceedingly rare in this part of the Western Reserve before the days of the Erie and Ohio Canals.

At social gatherings in the early days Jonathan must have sung the hymns everyone loved and also the tunes he brought along in his mind from Connecticut and written in his Ohio cabin. And on such occasions, of course, he also played his beloved violin.

How far Jonathan ranged as a teacher of church music we cannot be certain, but there is an amusing story in General Bierce's history that in Hudson none other than John Brown of Osawatomie was one of his pupils. In his usual earthy fashion, Bierce says that Jonathan found the big, gawky boy untidy and had to tell him to wipe his nose. This must have been soon after 1810, when John was ten, for he grew up fast and at the age of fifteen he was a full-grown man and soon after started a tannery. In 1820, John married Diantha Lusk of Hudson, daughter of the widow who is said to have taught in Jonathan's log cabin shop-and-school-house. Five years later the couple moved to Crawford County, Pennsylvania, the next step on the long, long trek which ended at Harper's Ferry.

But Jonathan had frequent business relations with John Brown's father, Owen Brown, who spent most of his life in Hudson after he moved there in 1805. Owen bought lime from Jonathan in 1820 and 1822, as we know. We also have a letter in Owen's hand written to Jonathan on June 21, 1832, which shows, incidentally, that Hale had friends and connections in Cleveland. It seems that Mercy Hale's father came to the Reserve in 1823, shipping his belongings from Buffalo to Cleveland in a vessel which belonged to Captain Levi Johnson. Johnson built the town's first ships, including the steamship "Enterprise", and he also built houses and the first Cuyahoga County Court House. Hale wrote to his friend Phineas Shepherd of Cleveland asking him to pay Captain Johnson the charge for transporting Father Piper's belongings. Shepherd passed the word to Captain Johnson, who in turn passed it to Owen Brown. But Brown forgot the matter until 1832, nine years later, when Captain Johnson brought it up. In embarrassment Owen got the money from Shepherd and then wrote to Jonathan Hale explaining what had occurred, asking him to reimburse Shepherd for the amount of $10.00 in charges and $6.32 in interest. The fault clearly lay with Brown and not with Hale.

VII

BUILDING "OLD BRICK"

1824 - 1827

On September 27, 1824, Jonathan Hale wrote an intriguing letter to his nephew Joseph Wright in Glastonbury. Unfortunately the letter is lost, and all we know of its interesting contents is the brief comment Joseph made in reply. He wrote Jonathan on February 14, 1825, including in his letter the following sentence: "You mentioned you were about to build a brick house and by your description a very nice one." Just what did Jonathan write?

This letter proves, of course, that Jonathan had begun to think about his house weeks or months before he sent its description to Joseph Wright. This is two years or more earlier than any date that appears in the family traditions about the house, which place its construction between 1826 and 1827. Undoubtedly both Joseph and the Hales are right, for to build the house he eventually did, Jonathan required not only hopes and plans but money and materials, and there were time-consuming problems involved in securing both.

Further on in his letter Joseph wrote that "If money is as scarce with you as it is here it will be a hard time to build." We know from Jonathan's accounts that what he called cash was increasing in the Valley, and Joseph himself had learned in 1820 that Jonathan was beginning to prosper. In a letter he wrote that year reporting on a visit from Elijah Hale, who had brought along all the news from the Valley, Joseph writes, "It seems you have a very good farm, much better than Uncle Elijah's; you also have a limestone quarry which promises to be very useful to you." Knowing Joseph's style, "useful" undoubtedly refers to profits.

Going back to the letter of 1825, Joseph also gives us a hint of the excitement which had begun to spread up and down the Cuyahoga Valley, one which Connecticut could not share. "You mention", he wrote, "about the proposed Canal that was to pass by your house. I think it would be beyond my calculations to estimate the advantage it would be to you and your country generally." The Cuyahoga country had vast hopes for the great Canal, and Jonathan naturally shared them. By September, 1824, when he wrote to Joseph about his house, the Canal Commissioners had reported in favor of a Cleveland-to-Portsmouth canal, and it was to follow the Cuyahoga from the Portage to the Lake. This clinched the matter, and it is not a coincidence that Jonathan was thinking of his fine big house at the very moment the Canal along the river was becoming a foreseeable fact.

And there were other reasons for Jonathan to think in 1824 of building a house. There is no doubt that by the standards of the Valley, he was a relatively prosperous man. The countryside was filling up with settlers, and canal or no, the future was bright. The family of seven had lived long enough in the crowded cabin Jonathan had inherited from Captain Miller, and it was no longer appropriate for the position Jonathan held in the little community. Seven years earlier Jason Hammond had built a small frame house down the road, and in the prospering farm land and villages of Tallmadge, Stow, Hudson, and Portage, comfortable white-painted frame houses were being built in the charming, classical style we know as "Western Reserve". It was derived from the Connecticut houses almost everyone in the countryside knew, but it had an elegance of detail and variety of plan that were mostly new.

Jonathan had the materials, the site, and a good deal of the simplest kind of craftsmanship to build something quite different. He had been born and brought up in a brick house with a gambrel roof in Glastonbury, built by his father and grandfather from brick they made on the site. Jonathan, of course, had been making brick in recent years from clay across the road and he could burn the lime he needed for mortar. His son William was now eighteen and Andrew thirteen, both old and strong enough to help. Even more important, Elijah Hale's daughter Eveline had married a talented young man from Sandisfield, Massachusetts, named John Bosworth.

Bosworth had come to Bath Township around 1820, and he and Eveline were married in her father's cabin the following year, moving a few months later to Rootstown, just to the south of Ravenna. He is important to us because as a boy he had been apprenticed to someone in the wood-working trade— a carpenter or a joiner. He brought to the Western Reserve the skills he had learned.

Tallmadge lies on the road between Bath and Rootstown, and it is almost certain that in this prosperous little town Bosworth met another Sandisfield man named Colonel Lemuel Porter. He had left Massachusetts a year or so before Bosworth was born, to become apprenticed to a joiner in Waterbury, Connecticut. Porter must have had unusual talent, for he was employed later by a maker of wooden-wheeled clocks. Significantly, one of his fellow workers was David Hoadley, who built some of the famous churches around New Haven and Waterbury.

In the spring of 1817 Porter moved his family west to Tallmadge, and in this growing community he found plenty of work. Before 1825 he had built a frame house for Reuben Beach, who bought two casks of lime from Jonathan, another for Asaph Whittlesey, also one of Jonathan's customers, and a third for Gerrold Wolcott, all prominent Tallmadge men. In Northampton, Porter also built a house for Aaron Norton, Jonathan's friend the miller. There were probably more.

In these early days, a craftsman like Porter grew from necessity to be more than just a carpenter and joiner. The work he did on a house—from laying the beams to making the window and door frames—lay at the center of the building operation. It was a natural process that Porter should become a carpenter-contractor-architect. He probably drew whatever plans he used, hired the masons and assistant carpenters, and supervised the entire job. He learned all this by doing it, one house after another, beginning in the towns of Connecticut.

It was natural enough that Porter should hire a young man with Bosworth's talents, for they were very rare in the Western Reserve. There was the tie with Sandisfield, through the Porter and Bosworth families if nothing else, and craftsmen engaged in the same line of work would inevitably drift together in such a sparsely settled community as the Cuyahoga country.

Bosworth's first work for Porter may well have been on the lovely Tallmadge church, one of the finest in the Western Reserve. In December, 1821, Porter was given a contract to "superintend the joiner work" and he hired a boss carpenter named Sebbens or Stebbins Saxton. A boss naturally assumes a crew, and one of these may have been Bosworth, who had married Eveline Hale a few months before.

We have no direct evidence that Bosworth worked for Porter, but after the latter's death, Bosworth built at least three churches in the vicinity. The first was the Rootstown church, built in 1829. It is described in a history of Portage County as "a very neat edifice for the time, which was 36 x 46 feet." His next church was in Ellsworth, now in Mahoning County, and the date was around 1835. The most interesting by far of the three was the handsome little church in Atwater, which he began in 1839. It was completed, without the present tower, after Bosworth's death in 1840. Authorities on the architecture of this period in the Western Reserve describe the church in Atwater as second in interest only to Porter's famous church in Tallmadge. They say that both these churches are equal or superior to the best that were built in New England during these years. The Atwater church, with its pointed windows, forecasts the Gothic revival and has been copied in a number of churches in this part of the Reserve.

The church at Tallmadge was not dedicated until 1825, and by then Jonathan Hale was deep in his hopes and plans for the new brick house in the Valley. It is likely that he and William and Andrew were making the brick and burning the lime the house would require. As far as we know, Jonathan's experience in building had been limited to the log barn and the sheds around his farm. He may well have learned to lay brick in Connecticut, just as he learned to make it. But there was far more involved in the project he had in mind than this.

Nor at the time was there another brick building in this part of the Western Reserve that could serve as a model. Whatever recollections of such houses he had from his Connecticut days, including the house in which he was born, were fifteen busy years behind him. Nor does the house Jonathan built resemble these Connecticut houses in important details of exterior design, the plan of the rooms, and the setting.

But in the spring of 1826 the new and struggling Western Reserve College in Hudson began the first building on its farm-land campus, to be known as Middle College. Colonel Porter was available for the job, now that the Tallmadge church was finished, and on March 3, 1826, he was given a contract by the College Trustees "for doing all the carpenter and joiner work." This meant that he supervised the entire job, and the College built a house in Hudson for the Colonel and his family so he would be close at hand. The building was to be fifty-six feet long and thirty-seven feet wide. The exterior was to be built of brick.

At about the same time these two brick buildings were being planned in Bath and Hudson, a third brick structure was probably in the planning or talking stage further north in the Valley. It stands today on Canal Road in the southeast corner of Independence Township and it was probably built by a man named Hynton. It was a large annex to a little two-story brick house he had put up around 1809, which is probably the oldest building now standing in the Cuyahoga Valley.

These three structures lie within twelve or fifteen miles of each other, and we know from Jonathan Hale's account books that contacts over such distances were frequently made. Furthermore, the buildings were extraordinarily similar in exterior design. It is not beyond reason to assume that one man influenced, at least, the building of all three, without necessarily drawing the plans. The most logical choice is Colonel Lemuel Porter.

All three buildings were long across the front, narrow and high, with sturdy chimneys at each end. The Hynton house is the smallest and plainest, only two stories high, with no ornament to speak of, and it may have been the model for the others. Middle College, which was unfortunately torn down in 1912, was somewhat more elaborate, four stories high, with lintels of stone in place of the simple brick ones on Hynton's house. The lintels Hale used are more elaborate still, brick with attractive little keystones in the center of each, somewhat crudely shaped from stone. The doorways of all three are like their windows, and none was surrounded by the framework of columns and moldings common in the wooden houses being built at the time.

Except perhaps for Hale's little keystones, none of the three brick buildings shows any trace of the Greek Revival influence which is so clear in the frame houses going up all around them. In fact the three resemble only each other. We know that Porter was contractor for Middle College, and that Bosworth did carpentry and joining for Jonathan Hale—and perhaps on Middle College as well. We know nothing of Hynton, but it seems logical that he consulted the best and nearest authorities around him, and these could have been Porter or Bosworth, or both.

*   *   *   *   *   *

Nothing as detailed as a modern blueprint could have been drawn for the Jonathan Hale house, and no one could be called its "architect" as the word is used today. As we have seen, the jobs of carpenter, joiner, contractor, and architect were more-or-less merged, and the true professional architect who only designed the building and drew the plans did not develop in the Reserve until around 1850. One of the earliest was Porter's son Simeon, who worked with his father in Tallmadge and Hudson and then formed a partnership in Cleveland with the well-known architect Charles Heard.

John Bosworth's daughter, the Eveline Bosworth Cook we have quoted before, recalled that her father built the stairways and cornices for Jonathan's house. In view of the churches he built a few years later, it seems likely that he did much more. He may well have made the sketches which were needed to establish the proportions of the house and lay out the rooms and windows, borrowing his basic ideas from Porter's work in Hudson, or even Hynton's on Canal Road. The brick walls of Middle College were going up in the summer of 1826, and this fits in with the Hales' traditional dates for the building of Jonathan's house, which are 1826 and 1827.

The brick, as we know, was made across the road. The wet clay was probably shaped in large forms and sliced with some sort of cutter. An oven-like structure of brick or stone could have served as a kiln. The process was crude and the bricks had serious flaws, which were certainly due to the clay. But the colors were rich and varied—from soft orange reds to dark mahogany tones which sometimes give off a hint of glass-like blue, from over-burning. Some of the light-colored bricks are almost powdery soft, and one can rub off the clay with a finger—though no one is encouraged to do so! There are small cracks and considerable roughness, and the edges are often irregular. As the years went by, the brick on the exposed side of the house crumbled away and was replaced. The original brick survives in the cellar behind the basement room and in part of the rear wall of the three-story house. But in color and texture, in spite of, or even because of, its flaws, Jonathan's brick has far more interest as a building material than modern, machine-made brick. He also achieved an open-work pattern and a lozenge design on the north end of the house, and courses between the floors across the front.

The brick in Jonathan's ancestral home in Glastonbury is very similar in appearance, but virtually all of it remains. Thanks to the quality of the clay —a factor over which, after all, Jonathan had no control—the brick is far superior, as he must have been aware. The exterior of the Glastonbury house has been whitewashed, like all these old brick houses in the town, but there is no sign of deterioration. In the basement and attic the old brick is easier to examine, and it has the same colors, shape, and attractive uneven texture as the brick in Bath. But none of it is "soft", to borrow the term Jonathan used in his accounts when he spoke of interior brick. To our knowledge, the clay which Jonathan burned for his house in the Valley was never used again.

The brick was probably laid by Jonathan, William, and Andrew, and they no doubt shaped the rough ceiling beams from logs they cut in the woods in the hillside. The flooring and smaller beams were probably sawn in one of the mills on Yellow Creek. For especially heavy jobs like cutting the stone for the cellar walls, hired help was probably used. But the Hales, perhaps with help from the Hammonds near by, did as much of the job as they could themselves. Eveline Cook, for instance, reports that years later her cousin William plastered some walls in her grandfather's house on the hill, and he may have learned this skill while helping his father.

The original homestead consists of the big, three-story section which faces Oak Hill Road and still dominates the rest of the house. Built into a slope, the first floor—called the basement—had no windows in the rear. The cooking was done on the great fireplace with its baking oven which fills the north end, though except for the mantel the present version is modern. It was an all-purpose "keeping-room", kitchen, dining room, and living room, reminiscent of the one big room in the old log cabin. But dividing it in the middle a stairway led to the second floor, rising beneath the present stairs which lead from the second floor to the third.

Behind and at the southern end of this fine big room a cellar was dug into the slope, and its original stone walls can still be seen. It was one step below the level of the adjoining room and about half as high, and the roof may have been covered with earth. It was used to store potatoes, apples, pork, firewood, and other supplies, taking the place of the little log building with a cellar beneath which stood between Hale Run and the cabin.

On the second and more formal floor, the stairs came up at the front of the house above the outside basement door, where a closet is now. The room to the north, or left, was the parlor for special occasions with an outside door on the side of the house for company. On the other side of the stairs was another attractive room which may have served at first as a dining room for formal occasions. Later it was Jonathan's bedroom and until 1902 it was the bedroom of Andrew's wife, Jane Mather Hale. It is furnished as a bedroom today.

Upstairs the original plan was strikingly different from the two rooms of the present house. There were no closets or bathrooms, naturally enough. But the two pleasant rooms we know today were divided for a time into no less than six and a narrow hall. To accomplish this feat, the room at the north was divided first by a wall that ran between the windows from east to west, with small doors at each end. Then each of the resulting rooms was divided again by a wall running north and south. In the room on the other side of the stairs a hall led back to a small attic above the addition to the house we shall mention soon, and another pair of rooms was formed by dividing the remaining space in half. The only heat in these minute little rooms came up the stairs from below, for there are no fireplaces on this floor.

For a number of reasons we shall discuss below it was possible around 1830 to remove the two partitions running north and south, leaving three comparatively spacious bedrooms. Stoves were probably installed in the two outside rooms using the chimneys as flues.

Surprisingly for these early years, an important addition was made to the house and for an important reason. William Hale and Sally Upson planned to be married and it was decided for the sake of economy that they should live for a time at least in the house. To help solve this housing problem, already acute, a living room to serve as a more attractive place than the basement for the family to gather, was added at the rear of the house with a small attic above it. To support it the stone walls of the storage cellar were raised by using the only important quantity of Jonathan's brick work which survives. William and Sally were married in the parlor on the second floor, and not to be confused with the more informal living room, in September, 1828, they moved into the basement. As Eveline Cook explains, the young couple "occupied the basement room, keeping house in it." The whole family necessarily had to cook and eat there too, and the living room was open to all.

The most interesting details of the interior of the house are three fine mantels, two on the second floor and one at the south end of the basement. These show workmanship beyond anything one could expect from Jonathan Hale. Nor were they inspired by any of the builders' handbooks which were so popular at the time, such as those by Asher Benjamin and Minard Lefever. They were done in the "vernacular"—the derived but handsome and largely amateur architectural language of the unknown craftsmen of the Western Reserve. In fact these three mantels alone in the original house show the influence of classical models which marks the best work of the early Western Reserve.

In their basic design these charming mantels are not unusual. Their fascinating feature is the small, ribbed or reeded panels, made with a beading plane, which are arranged in a variety of ways and sizes to fill the spaces between the moldings across the top and down the sides. Some of the panels have been pierced with holes near the top and bottom to vary the effect still further. It is probable that the mantels were built in the thirties, or at about the time William and his wife took over the basement quarters, for one of them graces the big room there and is obviously later than the simple old fireplace at the other end. It is possible that John Bosworth did the work, or had it done by the craftsmen who were helping him build his churches, though Andrew Hale, we know, also had a beading plane. These little panels seem to be unique in the surrounding countryside.

Other woodwork which has interest is that on the mantel above the north basement fireplace. It is a series of graceful but rather heavy moldings curving inward at each end. It is good, straightforward, and original work and might well have been done by Bosworth when he built the stairs and cornice.

The oldest and biggest hand-hewed beams in the house which can still be seen are those in the cellar off the basement room. Other original wood is the floor in the second-floor parlor and in the bedrooms on the third floor. These wide, yellow boards are poplar, with an occasional replacement of other wood. The outside doors in the basement and second floor of the old house are original, but the top wooden panels have been removed for glass. The old windows in the basement had 12 panels to a sash, those upstairs had nine, the oldest photographs of the house show. The Hynton house down the Valley has a few panes of original glass, handmade and showing wrinkles and other defects which today only add to its charm, and the glass in the Hale house was probably of similar quality. In Hale's account book he records that he bought 14 panes of glass, for use in the cabin, from Dr. Hudson for 10 cents a pane. Two years later, in 1822, he traded lime to one Normand Baldwin who probably lived in Hudson, "to be paid in goods or glass." It is likely that he bought the glass for his big new house from some such source as this.

One thing is certain: All the materials Jonathan used in building his house came from the land he owned or the surrounding townships—the same area, in fact, in which he had sold his lime. There is no reason to think that he imported his building supplies from Cleveland or the other towns on the new Ohio Canal, which opened for business while the house was under construction. Local craftsmen could supply his needs, and he tailored his requirements to fit what they could produce.

Nails, for example, he had traded for lime with Captain Thorndike and Martin Camp of Tallmadge several years before he began to build the house. He also obtained raw iron from Dudley Griswold and a Mr. Jerrod of Tallmadge and from Stephen Remelee of Portage in the same way. The iron door hinges and latches were probably cast in Tallmadge where the metal seems to have been plentiful, for there is no evidence that Jonathan cast them himself. Much of this handsome hardware is still in the house though some is carefully-made reproductions.

No precise date can be given for the completion of "Old Brick", as the family lovingly called it. In fact it grew for many years. The family may have moved from the cabin into the basement by the end of 1826, for it was probably in usable shape and likely to be warmer in winter. After that the upstairs rooms were used as soon as the building operations made it feasible. We know, however, that Sophronia, the oldest of the children, was married to Ward K. Hammond in May, 1827, before the parlor was plastered. In the fall of 1828 Pamelia married William Oviatt and William was also married, but nothing was reported about plaster.

It was these marriages which caused the early additions to the house. We know about the new living room which was probably still being built during the wedding festivities of Pamelia and William. Tragically, Sally died within a year of her marriage, but William soon married again and moved back to the basement. When Andrew married his step-sister Jane Mather in 1838, there was nothing for William and his growing family to do but build a house of their own across the road to ease the congestion. This was finished in 1840 and William moved out of "Old Brick." Andrew promptly moved into the basement, obviously from rooms upstairs.

Sometime during the forties, however, Andrew's family also outgrew the basement. He was devotedly attached to the house and its farm and rather than build another house he added a story-and-a-half frame wing to the basement on the south. The original door between the two buildings stands at the right of the mantel on the south wall of the room.

To continue the story of the growth of "Old Brick" into the later years, Andrew moved the wooden wing he had built around to the rear of the house, attaching it to the living room. It became known as the "south wing", and the change greatly improved the appearance of the house from the road. Still later a wooden "north wing" was built as a storage house for coal and other supplies, with a "corn room" above it. A small porch, which in a form somewhat enlarged now serves as the office of the museum, connected this wing with the rest of the house. These additions, too, in recent years have been covered with brick.

The white wooden porch on the front of the house replaces an attractive Victorian porch built in the late 1840s or 1850s. It had a hip roof with a scroll-work railing around it and more scroll work on the columns which held it up. The present porch is more in keeping with the style of the original house.

VIII

LIFE IN THE VALLEY

1825 - 1850

Inevitably, the history of the Hales and the Valley cannot be cut up into convenient units. In many cases the events and trends of the second quarter of the century begin before 1825 and continue on after 1850. But in general these years followed a pattern of unprecedented growth and change.

The period opens with the construction of the Ohio Canal. Its importance to the people who lived near its banks was undoubtedly great, especially in the towns and cities. But we learn from Eveline Bosworth Cook and General Bierce, who lived in these times, that in the twenties and thirties, much of the daily life in the small communities remained simple, earthy, and crude. For the place and the times, Jonathan Hale was a surprisingly cultivated man, but he was also a farmer and clearly at ease with his neighbors of all degrees. He liked the country banter and the sparse, laborious life.

The Ohio Canal was a matter of dollars and cents to a farmer like Jonathan Hale, for it provided him with a relatively easy, inexpensive access to markets far beyond the range of the surrounding towns in which he usually traded. Before the canal was built, there was no reason for Hale to expand his production of wheat, pork, beef, timber, and hay beyond the needs of the immediate community to which he sold, for transport by wagon to Cleveland, for instance, was costly and slow. Whether he did clear more of his land, sow larger crops, plant more apple trees, cut more timber, and raise more hogs and sheep after the canal was opened, we do not know, for these accounts have not come down to us. But it seems quite likely that he did. And just as important for the women of the Valley, the canal brought in, in slowly increasing quantities an assortment of goods from the eastern cities at prices they could now afford to pay.

The wave of canal building, as everyone knows, got its first great impetus in New York State, thanks to DeWitt Clinton and his Erie Canal. But canals were being discussed in the Western Reserve before Jonathan Hale arrived, and by 1818 the talk had turned into action. It was the deplorable and hopeless state of the roads which made the farmers and merchants yearn for a canal. Travel by water has always been cheaper than travel by land, and in these years it was infinitely easier.

The construction of the Erie Canal had barely begun when *The Cleveland Herald* reported in August, 1824, that Alfred Kelley, the indefatigable builder of the Ohio canals, had arrived at the Portage "and will immediately commence the location of a line of the Ohio Canal from that place to the still waters of the Cuyahoga," about five miles above the village of Cleveland. This was hopeful, wonderfully exciting news for the Valley.

A bill approving Kelley's survey of the canal from the Lake at Cleveland to the Ohio River at Portsmouth passed the legislature in February, 1825. The Canal Commissioners, of whom Kelley was by far the most active, were allowed to raise money by selling bonds in New York City. That spring experienced engineers were hired away from the Erie Canal and bids were taken for digging the ditch between Portage Summit and Cleveland. On the 4th of July ground was broken in a colorful ceremony at Licking Summit, and Governor Clinton of New York appropriately turned the first shovel of earth.

Kelley was immensely capable and he drove his men to the edge of endurance. As his contractors discovered, he was also incorruptible. Contracts for digging and banking the bed of the canal were let to local men, but, as we shall see, one of the Cozads of East Cleveland built locks north of Boston which required a greater skill. On July 22nd, *The Herald* reported that some 21 miles of the canal north of Portage Summit were under contract and "being prosecuted with great zeal." A few sections were "very nearly completed," though this could not have included the locks. "A great number of laborers are employed and every vessel from Buffalo brings more or less of the hardy sons of Erin seeking employment in the same business."

Like the Erie, the Ohio Canal was 40 feet wide at water level, 26 at the bottom, and four feet deep. The locks were 90 feet long, 15 to 20 feet wide, and the average lift was 10 feet. When it was finally finished to the Ohio River in 1832, the canal was 309 miles long and cost $4,695,203. Thanks to Kelley, this was far less per mile than the cost of the Erie.

The section between the Summit and Boston—the country of the Hales—was the first on the entire length of the canal to be built and opened. Jonathan and his family and neighbors made money out of the project, for the Irish laborers had to be fed and the work required the hiring and driving of teams and wagons.

O. W. Hale says the stone construction of the near-by locks supplied his grandfather with "a market for lime, a large quantity of which he burned and sold at this time." Unfortunately, this was a year or so after Jonathan made his last entry in the account books which still exist, so we have no record of these interesting sales. He may also have supplied from his forest land some of the oak and elm Kelley required for the piles to build the more difficult locks. There are four locks which could easily have been supplied from "Old Brick"—the one at Unionville, later known as "Johnny Cake Lock", as we shall see; "Pancake Lock", due east of the house; and a double lock a mile or so further south, near Botzum.

"There were a great many Irish employed," O. W. Hale goes on, "and many of them died from the bilious fevers that were so prevalent at the time. Quite a number"—a marginal note says 16—"were buried in the old burying ground . . . At one of their burials after they had deposited the remains and without ceremony heaped up the mound, one of their number said, 'There, be jabbers, if the half of us kin be buried as dasent as that man, we may thank the good Lord.' "

Work continued through the winter of 1825, in spite of the weather, and in April of 1826, *The Herald* wrote that "the canal line from this village to the Portage Summit presents a scene of industry and enterprise." That summer some 2,000 men and 300 teams were at work between Cleveland and Kendal, some twenty miles south of the Portage. Between Portage Summit and Cleveland there were 42 locks more-or-less under construction which dropped the canal 395 feet.

On July 4, 1827, the first canal boat, named "The State of Ohio," brought Governor Trimble and a party of distinguished guests down the canal from Portage Summit. There were cheering crowds, speeches, and "refreshments" along the way and one can be sure that a party of Hales and Hammonds saw the little vessel pass through the lock at Unionville. In Cleveland the Governor's party adjourned to Belden's Tavern where "dinner was served and the residue of the day was spent with good feeling." The following day the first commercial boat arrived in Cleveland with a load of whiskey and flour.

Jonathan Hale and his sons could not have worked very long on the canal, if they were employed at all, for they were busy burning lime. And in those very same years, 1826 and 1827, they were building "Old Brick". It is likely that the profit Jonathan made from his lime and from the use of his teams, went into the house—for paying the wages of men like Bosworth. And it is not beyond reason to think that he might have used one or two Irishmen as laborers when they were laid off from work on the canal.

Traffic grew slowly the first year, but trade through the port of Cleveland doubled in 1826. The great burden of traffic going north was flour and timber of various sorts, though whiskey, barreled pork and beef, cheese, lard, and stone were also shipped. The Hales and Hammonds could have shipped some of this, and what they did undoubtedly went through the warehouse at Unionville, their most convenient access to the canal by road and only a mile-and-a-half away. The southbound trade was in items like salt, barreled fish, finished lumber, and shingles. But more interesting to the women of the Valley were "merchandise" and "28 tons of furniture." Passengers going south were mostly settlers and outnumbered those going north by three to one.

The tolls as reported in *The Herald* seem moderate and were certainly cheaper than the cost of teaming to or from Cleveland. For flour, meat, grain, and most agricultural products the Hales and Hammonds were likely to ship, the rates were 1 cent 5 mills per ton-mile. Merchandise coming by the canal from the Lake—the welcome flow of dry goods, groceries, hardware, wrought iron and steel—paid 4 cents per ton-mile.

The village of Unionville, was created by the canal and by the lock on the site, which is still in good condition. Alanson Swan bought much of the land in the place and a building which had once been owned by the Iddings family. He seems to have had a warehouse, as well as a tavern for the entertainment of canalers and for passengers while their packets were locking through.

Goodspeed tells us in his history of Boston Township that "the village has been called 'Johnny cake' since 1828", the second year of the canal. "In the spring of that year, a flood in Furnace Run swept into the canal and stopped navigation, and the crews and passengers were compelled to live, water bound, as best they could. They were at last reduced to Johnny cake, which constituted their diet for a number of days. It has been asserted"—by General Bierce, in fact—"that one baking of Johnny cake in the early morning furnished the warm daily meal. The cake was warmed up for dinner," at noon, that is, "and served cold for supper." It is probable that the name "Pancake Lock" for the next one to the south was acquired in a similar way.

Over the years, the canal brought a new prosperity and an easier, more varied life to the people of the Valley. It raised the value of most of the surplus they had for sale by opening new markets as far east as New York City. By the late 1840's it brought the factory-made cottons and woolens of New England, and the furniture, household tools and utensils, and better farm equipment made in the factories of the old Connecticut towns. They could now buy scores of items they could not have made as well, or made at all. While the canal eventually destroyed much of the back-woods color of the early Valley and, what was worse, almost all of the handcrafts, it vastly broadened its horizon and made it far more aware of the outside world.

However, the canal was slow and tapped a limited market and when the rails began to be laid across Ohio during the 1850s, its future was clear. But for years no rails competed directly with the section of the old canal from the Portage to the Lake. It managed to survive even the Valley Railroad which was built in 1880, but finally surrendered to progress in 1924.

Today most of the canal can be traced from Cleveland to the Portage, though some short sections have been filled to build a road or some other modern convenience. In the country Jonathan knew so well it has suffered most of the damage, though the four locks can still be plainly seen. Today the canal seems surprisingly small and it takes imagination to remember the importance it had in the history of rural Ohio and the cities of Cleveland and Akron.

*   *   *   *   *   *

The primitive, back-country life of the little settlements in the Valley was doomed by the canal, but it by no means died overnight. As we shall see, Eveline Cook has preserved a great deal of this kind of life as it lasted on at a rather genteel level. On a quite different level, the broad and humorous myths and recollections of the Valley have come down to us from General Lucius Verus Bierce, a salty old character who fought in the wars against the British and Indians. He knew Jonathan Hale very well and has told us a few of the stories we know about him, and he also knew almost everyone else between Boston and the Portage. The facts in his history of Summit County are amusing but not reliable, and his manuscript had to be primly edited before it could be put into print in the year 1858. But the stories which survive in purified form, still give some of the gusty flavor of the times the General knew.

One of Bierce's favorite characters was Abner Robinson, who was famous in the Valley as a "poet." He flourished as late as 1840 in the vicinity of Johnny Cake Lock. Abner was "one of 'em," the General says. He had a trick of mixing up sentences for comic effect which Bierce calls his "crawfish manner of expression." Two pigs, for instance, "looked so much apart you couldn't tell 'em alike." This sort of comedy, and even more his verse, made Abner a local favorite and wit, and Jonathan knew him well.

Robinson's verse was extemporaneous and it is said that he never wrote it down. But it was sharp and apt and people remembered it. A good deal was aimed at evil doers, real or imagined—like Jacob Morter, known in Boston and along the canal for his alleged dishonesty. Hale himself had dealings with Jacob which turned out badly. Robinson's comic and lyric powers increased under the influence of megethlin, the powerful beverage made with honey, and the result of one of his bouts was a series of verses ending with this:

> Thus, Jacob Morter, as 'tis said,
> Steals all the corn that makes his bread.
> And while his neighbors are asleep
> The paltry scoundrel steals their sheep.

The language has undoubtedly been purified for print.

Alfred Kelley was unpopular because of his scrupulous honesty. While checking up on the rather dubious characters who dug the canal, he was in the habit of wearing a warm "blanket coat." The men around Johnny Cake Lock had no use for him, and Abner wrote:

> Old Beelzebub when he gets him there
> Will take him by the throat
> And hold him in the brimstone fire
> And singe his blanket coat.

Another upright man for whom Abner and his cronies had no love—and received none in return—was Billings Chaffee. Bierce says he was a worthy Justice of the Peace who was "often called upon to measure out Justice to Abner." He was also the follower of an unpopular political figure named Bliss. Abner's dissenting opinion was this:

> "My name is Billings Chaffee
> In Boston I do dwell,—
> There's not a neighbor in the town
> But wishes me in hell.
> They say that I am partial
> And all such stuff as this,
> That I've no judgment of my own
> But am controlled by Bliss.

As verse none of this is worth remembering, but as a bit of frontier life, we can be grateful that Bierce wrote it down. He also recorded amusing stories he heard up and down the Valley and one is about "Money Shop Hill", a name which older residents of the Valley remember and still use. "It was just over the line in Northampton and about a quarter of a mile from Jonathan Hale's." On it three brothers named Mallett—Henry, John, and Daniel—"manufactured currency to order." In other words "they erected a mint."

> This drew around the settlement a set of visitors that added anything but respectability to the place, and the inhabitants determined, if possible, to get rid of them. They accordingly called a council at the "money shop" in the absence of the workmen, when it was moved and carried to tear down the mint. Jonathan Hale, who dissented so far as to refuse aid to the work, turned his back on the building.

As he walked away, fire brands whizzed through the air and by morning the place was in ruins. Henry Mallett, however, continued "tinkering with currency" until he landed in jail in Columbus.

One reason Jonathan may have walked away was the fact that he had bartered goods and services with the Malletts in his early days in the Valley, and it was Henry who had bought his violin!

*　　*　　*　　*　　*　　*

There is a good deal more of this sort of thing in Bierce's book, but very little involved the Hales. However, in the family papers there is significant material in regard to some utterly different aspects of life in the Valley—the church and the school—and also some interesting hints as to the sort of books and periodicals the family read.

Life in Glastonbury had centered for almost a century around its Congregational Church. The town and the church were very nearly identical. But the power and influence of the New England churches had waned before the Revolution, as new political and philosophical ideas began to compete with the old theology. By 1810, when Jonathan and his family came to the Valley, religion had become a private rather than a political matter.

The Hales and Hammonds who lived in Bath were all deeply religious, but for the first thirteen years after they settled there, no formal church was established. There were several reasons for this. The towns of Connecticut had always been compact settlements compared to the scattered farm and villages of the Western Reserve. The people of the three river towns were a homogeneous lot, in origin and religious belief. The settlers in the West came not only from Connecticut but increasingly from the other states of New England and the Atlantic Coast. They brought a variety of faiths and the result was a greater religious freedom. Having survived the hardships of the early years without a church or a preacher, these devout people turned more and more to a personal religion and the Bible. The history of the Congregational Church in Bath proves, it seems, that old-school orthodoxy was a thing of the past.

The first formal religious service in Bath was probably held in 1818, the year the Township was incorporated. It was led by the Reverend Israel Shaler, or Shailer, a young Congregational missionary. In these years the Congregationalists and the Presbyterians had formed a rather uneasy alliance, under what was called the "Accomodation Plan." The first Congregational Church in Bath, for instance, was for many years under the supervision of the Presbytery of Huron.

The first couple the Reverend Shaler married in Bath were none other than John Bosworth and Eveline Hale, in 1821. Two years later a church was finally organized in the "Centre School House" at what is now called Bath Center. Andrew Hale was the last secretary of this little church, sadly closing its books in 1867 for lack of members. Fortunately he kept the records, and the two small volumes have been preserved in the family papers.

The most important of these little books contains the "Records of the Congregational Church in Bath organized November 24, 1823." Later it was known as the First Congregational Church. It was organized by three missionaries, Caleb Pitkin, John Seward, and Israel Shailer, or Shaler. Nine members of other churches "presented themselves with a request to be organized into a Church of Christ. As a preparatory step, the council," the missionaries, that is, "proceded to an examination of those persons respecting their doctrinal and experimental knowledge of the Christian religion and their vows of the duties and privileges of a Christian Church. Having gained satisfaction on these subjects the council proceeded to organize the church." The same sort of examination, but by the church itself, was held in open meeting whenever a new member joined a Congregational Church.

For the first ten years meetings were held in the "centre school". Most of the founding members transferred from churches in Stow and other nearby communities, but one was described as "Mrs. Mary Hale from the church in Glastonbury, Conn." This can only be Mercy Hale.

No other member of the Hale family joined the church during Mercy's lifetime, perhaps for the reason that the Center was too remote from the Valley in those early days. It is probable, too, that Jonathan was teaching music and leading the choir in one or the other of the older churches in the countryside during most of this period, and that the rest of the family joined him on Sunday. Also, the Hales may have gone to the church in the Center without becoming members.

But the Hammonds who lived up the hill near Hammonds Corners joined shortly after Mercy. In 1824 Calvin Hammond's wife Roxanna became a member and two years later her husband and Theodore Hammond followed along. Theodore, particularly, remained active in the church until he moved to the West in the 1850s.

As we shall see, Mercy died in 1829 and the following year Jonathan married Sarah Cozad Mather. She had been active in the Congregational Church affairs at her home in what was then called Euclid, now the University Circle area in Cleveland. Two years after her marriage, the church in Bath built a "meeting house" of its own, also in the Center. While it was under construction, the records show that on July 18, 1832 "Sarah Hale from Church in Euclid" became a member.

There is a story that William and Andrew helped build the new church, which held its first meeting on July 6, 1833. If so, neither one was a member, for on May 17, 1834, the record reads "Jonathan Hale, William Hale and Hariot his wife, Lewis Hammond and Morris Brown presented themselves for admission to this Church. Church proceeded to examine them. Expressed themselves satisfied . . . and voted that they be admitted into the Church the coming Sabbath." Andrew was admitted in 1836, and from that time on the Hales were dominant members of the little congregation. Jonathan, William, and Andrew served as delegates to the annual meetings of the Presbytery. When the church was incorporated in 1838 under a new law passed by the Legislature, William became a Trustee and held the post for years. Andrew became Secretary in 1847, holding the job until the end.

One surprising thing about this little church—whose membership at its height was only 64—is its concern with the morals of some of its members. To deal with such delicate yet public matters, special meetings were usually called to judge such crimes as adultery, fornication, drunkenness, violation of the Sabbath, and, of course, the sin of heresy. A dozen or so of the members were expelled, including a group of three argumentative heretics, but others confessed their crimes in open church and were allowed to remain. There is a comparatively mild reminiscence here of the unbelievable moral codes of the earliest New England churches.

The First Church of Bath faded away in the fifties and sixties, in good part for a curious reason. Its older members, including a number of Hammonds, joined a new migration to the West—this time to Illinois and the country to the West beyond the Mississippi. As a result, an increasing number of members asked the church for letters of transfer. It is probable, too, that the old-church Congregationalism which had apparently lived on in the church in Bath, repelled the younger generation. The Civil War seems to have been the final blow. On December 14, 1867, Andrew Hale, who was still the Secretary of the Corporation, made his final sad and significant entries. They were both in Andrew's difficult style, with spelling and syntax which do not speak well for the early schools of the Valley. The first of these two entries reads: "By previous appointment a meeting was held at Theodore Hales," as often happened in these final years of the church, "and letters were granted of dismission to Phineas Nash, Mary Vansickle and Pamelia Oviatt." Nash had been the first secretary of the church and Pamelia was Andrew's sister, the baby who made the journey in the wagon from Connecticut. The Oviatts were moving west. Closing his minutes, Andrew added, "There is only three male members now remaining this church perhaps the last letters given by this church." They *were* the last letters, for this was the end.

* * * * * *

It was an old failing on the part of the State of Connecticut that it did not require the Connecticut Land Company to reserve part of its land for the endowment of schools. The state may have expected the company to follow of its own accord the example of the Ohio Land Company, just to the south, which had assigned one-sixteenth of its land to the schools. The lapse is especially strange because the funds which the state received from the Connecticut Land Company were to be used for this purpose alone. In fact, the fund is still producing income today, though few Connecticut people are aware of the debt their children owe to the first settlers of the Western Reserve.

But the Company took no action, and the problem of supplying schools and teachers fell to the people of the little communities all over the Reserve. As a result, the growth of educational facilities was usually haphazard. According to Eveline Cook, the first school in Hammondsburgh was held in Aaron Miller's cabin in 1811—probably after he had moved to another in Boston—

and twenty-year-old Rachel Hammond, who had driven her father's wagon all
the way from Glastonbury, was the first teacher. However, the most reliable
historian of the township, W. A. Goodspeed, while he agrees that the first school
was in Miller's cabin, which he says was 16-feet square, claims that the first
teacher was Maria Lusk. She was a Hudson widow, the mother of the Diantha
Lusk who married John Brown. Rachel seems a more likely prospect, for she
lived a half-a-mile away. Goodspeed goes on:

> The first term was held in 1811, and after that date schools were
> held quite regularly in the neighborhood, sometimes in one house,
> sometimes in another, depending for location on the proximity of
> the greatest number of children . . . Alfred Wolcott [who had sur-
> veyed Jonathan's road] was one of the earliest teachers . . . A very
> early school was held in Mr. Hammond's house . . . Schools were
> usually taught by subscription and at stated time teachers were ac-
> customed to send their bills for collection.

For a year or so school seems to have been held in the very small log
house, also used as a shop, in front of Jonathan's cabin. Schools continued to
be taught in this oddly casual way in the northeastern corner of Bath until
1830, when a little building, also 16-feet square, was put up for the purpose.
"And the first teacher," Goodspeed says, "as far as we can ascertain, was Edward
Brown, a nephew of John Brown."

Sophronia Hale was seven when she made the journey from Connecticut
and may have had a year of schooling in Glastonbury, but the other four—
William, Pamelia, Andrew, and James Madison—were either too young to go
to school in Connecticut or were born in the Valley. We have evidence of the
quality of the teaching they had. Andrew's record books for the church are not
inspiring, but the accounts he kept for the farm at about the same time show
adequate spelling.

We do have two little books which belonged to William and two more
that were given to Pamelia. One of William's was a gift from a neighbor in
Glastonbury who bought it in 1809. Mercy may have read it to the four-year-old
boy as they rode in the wagon. It was a typical gift for a child of the times:
"The PIOUS PARENT'S GIFT:, or a PLAIN and FAMILIAR SERMON,
wherein the principles of the CHRISTIAN RELIGION, are proposed and
clearly represented to the Minds of CHILDREN, interspersed with APPRO-
PRIATE ENGRAVINGS, each of which is accompanied with Select Verses
from the Works of Dr. Watts." This was the work of William Mason and was
printed in London, without a date. The engravings are charmingly naive and
so is the prose. William's other book is a "Medley", printed in New York in
1815. Its size is only 2½ inches by 4 inches, and it contains little pieces about
birds and animals, a tale about "the enterprising traveler, Mungo Park," which
ends with an anti-slavery verse, and the usual delightful engravings.

The older of Pamelia's little books is the rather silly "Observations of Little Tommy Thoughtful," printed in Hartford in 1815. It deals with "the different tempers, genius, and manners of the young masters and misses in the several families he visited," and is not particularly appropriate for the Cuyahoga country.

Pamelia's other book is by far the most interesting of the four. It is an 1822 edition, a "revised impression, with the latest corrections," of Noah Webster's classic spelling book. With his usual wave of the flag, he called it "The American Spelling Book; containing the rudiments of the English language for the use of the schools in the United States." Webster's original edition had appeared in 1803, and with continuing changes it went on long after 1822. Pamelia dated her copy on December 18, 1822, when she was fourteen years old.

Webster begins with the "Analysis of Sounds in the English Language," which is remarkably lucid in spite of its difficult subject, goes on to the alphabet, the pronunciation and spelling of words from the polite four-letter ones to "im-pen-e-tra-bil-i-ty." There is also a small section on carefully selected French. To illustrate his text, Webster included fables and other brief pieces of running prose as well as the engravings usual in the books of the time. It was these little books and Webster's "Dictionary" which standardized America's spelling and much of its speech. Their immense influence on the American language cannot be measured, and it is typical of the range of the speller that it was used in Bath.

All told, these four assorted little books give us a small cross-section of the kind of reading the children did in the old log cabin, and later the big brick house. We have even less information about the literary fare of the older generation, for no one has bothered to record this phase of life in the Valley. But in the letters of Joseph Wright and Jehiel Hale we do have hints as to what Jonathan read and what his interests were. Though he must have read verse, for as we shall see he wrote a good deal, it was newspapers and magazines dealing with religion and politics which seem to have interested him most.

In January, 1814, Jehiel wrote Jonathan a letter in which he remarked, "I send you the 'Mercury' regularly but I know not whether you have received any of them". Three years later, Joseph brought up the matter: "I had supposed that you received a paper from Jehiel. I remember he sometime ago sent you the 'Mercury' & did not know but it was still continued. While adverting to this paper I would state that the bitterness of party has very much abated in Connecticut." Whether Jonathan received the paper we do not know.

The *Mercury* was actually the Hartford *American Mercury*, the Jeffersonian rival of the Federalist Hartford *Courant*, a paper which still exists. This could only mean that Jehiel and Jonathan were Jeffersonians, and this is supported by the fact that Jonathan named his youngest son, who was born in 1815, James

Madison Hale. To be a Jeffersonian in Connecticut in the days of the Embargo took courage, and dissatisfaction with New England Federalism may have influenced Jonathan's emigration to the West.

In the letter in which Joseph mentioned the *Mercury,* he also referred to other journals of considerably greater importance. He wrote on January 7, 1817, "I perceive by your letter that you have enjoyed the two best sources in the *political & religious* world—the National Intelligencer & the Panoplist."

The *National Intelligencer* was founded in Washington in 1800, serving as a weekly, semi-official reporter of the debates in Congress and other events in Washington. It was virtually the only source for this important news. It was a non-partisan paper until the time of Jackson, when it turned to the Whigs. In 1813, it became a daily, which makes it more remarkable that Jonathan read it. It may have been passed along by friends in Hudson or Tallmadge, though it is possible, of course, that he subscribed. In any event, it shows that Jonathan had a serious interest in politics. A little account book kept by William Hale has a list of nine voters, apparently those in the northeast corner of Bath, with their political affiliations. The Liberty, or anti-slavery, Party was alive, so the date falls between 1839 and 1848. There were seven Whigs, including Jonathan, Andrew, and William Hale and Lewis and William Hammond, one Liberty Party man, and a Loco-foco, a current nickname for Democrats. The Republican Party was founded in 1854, the year of Jonathan's death, and it was joined by the majority of Northern Whigs, including the Hales and Hammonds.

The monthly with the odd name of *The Panoplist* was a Congregational missionary journal founded in Boston in 1805. Jonathan's grandson says he subscribed that year. Its full name for the following three years was none other than *The Panoplist, or the Christian's Armory,* referring to the panoply or armor worn by a knight. In 1817, when Joseph mentioned it, the paper was called *The Panoplist & Missionary Magazine.* Four years later it took the simpler name of *The Missionary Herald* and Jonathan read it for the rest of his life. In his will he still referred to the "Panoplist and Missionary Herald".

*   *   *   *   *   *

The family moved into the big brick house late in 1826 or early in 1827, as we have seen. Housekeeping was much easier for Mercy, but her health was poor and she lived to enjoy her new surroundings only a couple of years. She was a thoughtful, kindly mother, wife, and friend, as gentle as her name. Andrew told Eveline Cook that after some "misdemeanor" of his, Mercy would remark, "Probably I shall punish you in the course of a week."

We have some touching evidence of the affection Jonathan bore for Mercy and she for him. For some reason, perhaps because it was a tender annual custom, on New Years Day, 1828, they wrote each other verses. We know that Jonathan wrote others, but the one we have of Mercy's is the only surviving evidence that she wrote them too. It should be remembered that the written exchanges of love and affection in these quite formal years mean more than they do today. "Friend" is commonly used for a husband or wife, and of course in conversation Jonathan was "Mister Hale". It is likely that the chief inspiration for these verses was the hymns they knew so well, though later rhymes of Jonathan's show that he must have read some of the popular verse of his day. Here is Mercy's:

> Jonathan Hale my companion & friend
>   I will pray for his happiness till life has an end,
> That when he retires from this earthly abode
>   His soul may be received to the mansions of God.

Jonathan's are equally formal, and one wonders whether he wrote tunes for them:

> Mrs. Mercy Hale, she is my true and loving wife.
>   She's been a slave to me a great part of my life.
> I hope she'll be rewarded here before she dies
>   And then receives a Mansion in Heaven above the skies.
>
> Her hands were always ready to smooth our pillows down
>   And always took great care of her little ones around.
> She always loved her husband as I do believe
>   and in return to her, the same from us receive.

As Mercy's health slowly began to fail, she yearned to see Connecticut and her family once more. It is a sign of the enormous improvement in the means of travel during the previous nineteen years that the trip was considered at all. Jonathan and Mercy went by packet to Cleveland on the new Ohio Canal, traveling by night. Jonathan, by the way, now spelled it "Cleaveland". There they boarded a schooner, and Jonathan tells the story in a letter he wrote to Wiliam on the "Eclipse", "off Buffalo May 27, 1829."

> My dear Son:
>   Agreeable to promise I shall write a few lines, to inform you that we arrived in Cleaveland the next morning after you left us [,] after a sleepless night about 10 o'clock [in the morning], & Sunday in the afternoon went aboard the schooner Eclipse Capt. Patterson and after being becalmed two days we are now in sight of Buffalo. Your Mother I think is no worse but rather better, as [she] sleeps better nights except the first.

As usual, Jonathan keeps a careful record of his expenses, and the contrast again is striking.

> I paid 1.75 for our passage to Cleaveland, $3.00 to Buffalo, and how I shall make out on the N. York canal I know not, but expect to be carried for a cent, or cent & a half a mile, about 300 miles, to Albany—We have been having good accomodations so far, and I ex-

pect to take passage in a canal boat to day or to morrow. I shall write
Mr. Oviatt next [a formal address for a son-in-law], and will inform
Pamelia & Sophronia how we have got along. I shall probably write
at Albany if not before. Your Mother thinks you had better let your
Aunt [Elijah's wife] have that Hanford wool.

Jon^a Hale

The letter is postmarked "Cleaveland" and had returned from Buffalo by
ship on June 8th. The promised letter to William Oviatt was written four days
earlier, on June 4, from Albany. If the canal boats were slow, the mail from
Buffalo to Cleveland was much slower.

My Dear Children:

Agreeable to promise I shall write a few lines, in haste of course
& be very brief. Your Mother has stood this Journey better than I
expected. Still she is subject to those painful turns. She is impatient
to get into the salt water which I hope by the day after tomorrow;
we was becalmed on the Lake 2 or 3 days, and some hindrance
[on] the N. York canal. I got passage from Buffalo to this place for
one cent a mile 363 amounting to $7.28 with pretty good accomoda-
tions.

This may refer to the passage and food on the Erie, for if Jonathan means
the total fare he has already mentioned on the Ohio Canal, the Lake, and the
Erie Canal, the amount is $8.38. He goes on:

I think I shall start from Albany tomorrow the Lord permitting. Our
present calculation is to sleep at Milford [Connecticut, east of the
mouth of the Housatonic] to take the benefit of the sea air, as well
as its products, but in that I may be frustrated, I know not the designs
of Providence in this Journey, but I pray that we may be restored to
health & be permitted to return to our children and friends. You
probably will see William or some of our family. You will let him
know how it is with us. The next letter I shall write to Ward [Ham-
mond, Sophronia's husband] probably from Connecticut when I shall
be more particular. We feel very troubled about Sally [William's wife,
Sally Upson, who by this time was desperately ill] and the rest of our
children. I hope they will see to all things. I know not how they will
manage affairs but have reason to believe they will get along very
well—*June 5th* I shall start in about two hours in the steam Boat for
New York, we have had some oysters by paying 12½ cents a dozen
& now I [am] going to Breakfast on a shad. Yours in great haste
etc., etc.

Jon^a Hale

Sally Upson Hale died on June 25th, and three days later, from Tallmadge, William wrote his parents about it. Allowing for stops, they must have
reached Glastonbury by the 15th. It is a heart-broken letter and the scene at
her death and her calm acceptance of the Saviour are described in great detail.
But he also found time to report that "the wheat looks very well but the corn,

flax, oats and grass will be very high . . . our meadows are very light but nothing in comparison to some others."

We have no more letters describing the trip, but Jonathan probably received William's letter before the end of July. This bad news and Mercy's continuing illness made it wise to start for home. On the Erie Canal Jonathan suffered a serious accident. As O. W. Hale puts it in his biography of Jonathan, "On getting up one night while on the canal boat for something for his sick wife, who grew worse while away, he slipped on deck and falling was caught on an iron hook, which tore an ugly gash in his thigh." We know from a letter written by Jonathan's cousin Joseph Welles that Jonathan himself referred to the accident as one he had "met with by the towline of the Canal boat." It may have been this which made him slip on the deck.

Somehow or other, the sadly ailing couple managed to reach the Valley in August. Mercy's health grew steadily worse and Jonathan's wound healed very slowly. Mercy died in the middle of October and her husband was still too sick to attend the funeral. She is buried in the little grave yard down Oak Hill Road, with so many other Hales and Hammonds.

*   *   *   *   *   *

Mercy's death was a fearful blow to Jonathan. There is sound evidence, in fact, that because of his grief he planned to leave the Valley and "Old Brick", and made arrangements to do so. The records of what was then Medina County show that about two months after Mercy's death Jonathan sold all of his Lot 13, mostly wooded and difficult land, to his oldest child Sophronia and her husband Ward K. Hammond for the moderate sum of $400. The following June, 1830, he disposed of the heart of his farm, meadow, and orchards in Lots 11 and 12 to his oldest son William, who was still a widower, for $2,100.

However, that fall Jonathan changed his mind, and it was probably a woman who convinced him to do it—that his ties to the Valley and his children and kinfolk should not be broken. She was an attractive and capable widow, living in what was then East Cleveland, named Sarah Cozad Mather.

Sarah Cozad was a very different sort of woman from Mercy Piper. She was the daughter of Samuel and Jane McIlrath Cozad and was born in Morris County, New Jersey, March 11, 1799. Thus she was twenty-two years younger than Jonathan. The family moved to Washington County, southwest of Pittsburgh, the following year and in 1806 moved again to the vicinity of Doan's Corners in Euclid Township, in what is now the University Circle area of Cleveland. Her father bought most of the land between Doan Brook and Lake View Cemetery and her brothers owned land across the street, including that between East 107th Street and Ford Drive. Sarah had a good education and

her family were distinguished members of the little community around Doan's
Corners.

In 1817 Sarah married William D. Mather—no relation, apparently, to the
more famous Mathers—whose family had settled in Boston and Northfield
Townships. Jonathan Hale sold lime, in fact, to an Elijah Mather of Northfield and a Waters Mather lived near Unionville. William took his bride to
a "rented farm" in Northfield Township and there three children were born—
George in 1819, Jane in 1821, and Betsey in 1823. Sarah also adopted an
orphaned child of her sister Anna, a girl named Harriet Carlton who played
an important role in this story.

In 1824 the family moved to the little crossroads of Unionville only a
mile-and-a-half from the log cabin of Mercy and Jonathan Hale. The families
became close friends. William Mather bought a farm "mostly on the river
bottom" where the Canal was built a year or so later. But during their first year
on the land the family was struck by the "billious fever", probably malaria,
and William died of it. He was buried in Boston Cemetery but Sarah was too
ill of the fever to attend the services. O. W. Hale tells us that "they lived
in a double house," which they shared with another family, "and grandfather
Hale's people attended the funeral."

Sarah recovered and bravely took her three small children back to Doan's
Corners, living with her widowed mother until Mrs. Cozad's death a few weeks
later. Sarah then moved in with her brother Nathaniel, in a house on the
north side of Euclid Road about on the site of the Claud Foster Dormitory
of Western Reserve University. But the following year Sarah returned briefly
to the Valley when another brother contracted to build some of the locks on
the new canal, north of Boston. Sarah kept house and boarded her brother's
hired hands, mostly Irishmen fresh from the Old Country and an unruly lot
indeed. No doubt she renewed her acquaintance with the Hales who were
finishing their new brick house.

The canal job was finished late in 1827 and Sarah went back to Doan's
Corners, teaching school and doing house work for the neighbors. But she was
prosperous enough to build a small brick house for her family on her father's
land, perhaps where Abington Road is today. She also founded a Sunday
School, the first in the area, which later grew into the Euclid Avenue Congregational Church, now at Euclid and East 96th.

Sarah was leading this useful and busy life when Mercy Hale died in
October, 1829. It was only two months later that Jonathan sold Lot 13 to
Sophronia and her husband. He may have planned to move to Cleveland,
which was having a boom thanks to the new canal, and perhaps while sur-
veying his prospects there he renewed his acquaintance with Sarah Mather.
His plans were still uncertain when he sold his remaining land to William in

June, but between then and November he decided to stay in Bath. For on November 2, 1830, Jonathan Hale married Sarah Cozad Mather in the parlor of her father's old house, which stood about on the site of the old Hatch Library on the campus of Western Reserve University.

As far as we know, the couple returned at once to "Old Brick". A few weeks later Jonathan wrote a long, romantic, and confusing poem which exists today in his own hand:

> To my Dearly Beloved Wife
> Mrs. Sally Hale — by Jonª Hale
> Dec. 12, 1830

It seems to show that there were emotional problems involved on Sarah's part and that she mourned for her friends, who were undoubtedly more sophisticated than anyone she could know in Bath, and for the familiar sights along Doan Brook and around the Corners. The poem is called "To a stranger", significantly enough, and in an amateur poetic style borrowed from the highly-colored romantic verse which was printed in the newspapers and magazines of the day, Jonathan tries to make his bride feel at home in her new surroundings while recalling her old ones. However, the last verse suggests that if she is still unhappy she should go back home and "lull thy lone spirit to rest." All we know is that Sally stayed on in "Old Brick" with every apparent sign of happiness.

In the poem, which is crude but quite delightful, Jonathan spells "thee" as "the". The "limpid rill" refered to is undoubtedly Doan Brook, quaintly enough and Sally's "favorite hill" may well be Ambler Heights.

To a stranger

Far from the land that gave the birth!
O! Canst thou find a spot on earth,
　　So fondly dear to the
As the heart-woven land thou hast left behind
In the earlyest wreath of young memory entwined,
With the friends and thy childhood that charmed the so long
With the soft mellow tones of their juvenile song
　　In the strains of affectionate glee.

Thou seest no more that limpid rill
Which purled beneath thy favorite hill;
　　Ah! wilt thou love to stray
In thy—lesness (?) now, by a strange streamlets side?
Wilt thou feel in thy bosom that innocent pride
Which stole on the so oft, when the light of its spell
Gave new charms to the dewdrops that lusciously fell
　　On thy own, thy loved path far away.

Thou'st left behind thy social train;
Will thy fond spirit rest again,
   And feel security
In the bosom of strangers thou ne'er has tried,
By the ebb and flow of prosperity's Tide
Or will it retreat on the soft wings of regret
To that frequented bower where so lovingly met
   All by friendship made sacred to the.

Believe me hear are friends as kind
As those whom thou hast left behind
   Green walks and streams that flow
With a current as clear and a murmur as soft
As that which has filled thy rich musings so oft,
O! then sever thy-self from the chanes of the past
With which thy affections are fettered so fast
   Since the present has gifts to bestow.

But canst thou not the fairy chase,
Which binds the to thy native place;
   Rather than be unblest,
To the friends of thy children—thy country thy home
Go—go and be happy, tis folly to roam,
Return to the shades of thy fair dropping vine
Where the pulses of nature are wedded to thine.
   Go and lull thy lone spirit to rest.

It may have been Sarah's inability to adjust herself to life in the Valley which led Jonathan to put off buying back the land he had sold to his children until 1833, which is the year these deeds were dated.

But Sarah must have been too busy to brood for long. Her oldest son, George Mather, was eleven when his mother re-married, four years younger than James, the youngest of Mercy's children. Jane Mather was nine and Betsey seven. Sophronia and Pamelia Hale had married and moved away, but William, Andrew, and James were still living at home. It is no wonder the bedrooms upstairs were so oddly partitioned off.

Somehow or other, Sarah found room in the house for her niece and adopted daughter Harriet Carlton, an attractive, capable young lady by now in her early twenties, who came to live in the house to help with the sewing and other chores. William promptly fell in love with her and he and Harriet were married in less than a year. They took over the basement where William and Sally Upson had lived so briefly, and there Harriet gave birth to her first two children, Sarah and Lucy.

This marriage tied the two families closely together, and the bonds became even closer when three children of their own were born to Sarah and Jonathan —named Jonathan, Mercy, and Samuel. For a couple of years there were fourteen Hales and Mathers living somehow in the big house, and they had to double up in the six improvised bedrooms upstairs.

It is significant of the friendly relations between the two women that Sarah, or Sally as she was usually called, gave the name Mercy to the only daughter she bore to Jonathan. O. W. Hale, a son of William and Harriet, has written of Sally that "no woman ever stepped into a vacant place that was abler filled than the one she stepped into. She was very kind and patient, and not withstanding the mixed lot of children, harmony and happiness reigned supreme." Eveline Cook says much the same.

As a final tie to knit the families together, Andrew Hale married his stepsister Jane Mather in 1836. Two years later, obviously from necessity, William and Harriet moved from the crowded brick house into a new frame one across the road. Andrew and Jane took over the basement room, and when their own family began to grow they added the wooden wing to the south of the house a few years later.

*   *   *   *   *   *

A great deal of interesting and important material has been collected or written concerning the homely details of everyday life in rural America before the Civil War. However, almost all of it is either too general or too local in nature to apply with certainty to the Cuyahoga Valley. Fortunately, we have the delightful memoirs written at the age of eighty by Eveline Bosworth Cook, which we have referred to many times. Looking back, she recalled the humble, completely unvarnished facts of her early life. She adds no romantic gloss to anything, and as a result she wrote an honest, important record, which pertains to the Valley and the lives of the Hales and the Hammonds, particularly in the 1830's.

In spite of a meager education, Eveline was an alert, intelligent girl. She was born in Rootstown in 1826. Her mother died soon after her birth, and her father, John Bosworth, the carpenter-architect, wisely decided that the child should be placed with her mother's family. Her grandparents were Sarah and Elijah Hale, who still were living in the log cabin they built on top of the hill. In her memoirs Eveline wrote that in her final illness her mother "gave" her to her sister, who was Eveline's Aunt Mary and also lived in the cabin. Eveline thought of her as a mother. At the age of twelve, Eveline was sent to Rootstown to live with her father and his second wife. But John Bosworth died two years later, and the child was sent back to her grandparents. At the rather advanced age of 26, she married James Cook, about whom we know nothing at all, and she died in 1908, two years after writing her memoirs.

All told, she lived for 22 years among the Hales and Hammonds. She went to whatever schools there happened to be in Bath or Rootstown. To judge by her memoirs her schooling was brief and her knowledge of written English was primitive. But this gives her reminiscences an added interest, for she obviously wrote pretty much as she spoke, with no personal pronouns, for instance, unless absolutely required for the sense. She recorded the stories she heard from her family and friends as well as her own observations of the life about her.

Eveline tells us much about the work around the house which she saw or helped to do, but there are important bits about other activities too. The work inside and out was hard, and for the Elijah Hales more primitive for a longer time than it was for the more prosperous families down in the valley. But it was varied by family reunions, by music, and the church. One gets the clear impression from Eveline's text that the lives of the Hales and Hammonds were tied closely together, from necessity and because they wanted to have it that way. As a result, she tells us almost as much about Uncle Jonathan Hale as she does about her nearer kin, on the hill.

A great deal of the time of the women in the families was spent in spinning, weaving, and sewing, for they bought few things "ready made." Even when the canal made them available, the women bought few "fancy dresses" from the local stores. Except for cotton, which did not appear in daily use until after the canal brought down the price, the raw wool and flax came from their own woodlands and fields. From about 1830 on, however, some of the processing of wool was done in "factories" in Ghent. All the rest of the work was done in their fields and kitchens.

Eveline's grandfather had more flax than wool, though the opposite was true of Jonathan—due to the cost of buying and feeding sheep. Jonathan, like the later Hales, pastured sheep in the woodlands which climbed the hill, where they fed on the young trees and the underbrush, leaving the great forest giants which stand there today.

"My grandparents done good deal hard work," Eveline wrote in her abbreviated style. "Among the rest was raising up flax. Think grandfather raised a good deal, had it rotted, then with his break got the wooden part of the stalk off." A "break" was actually a brake, a sturdy wooden frame about five feet long standing on four legs. The stalks of flax were placed across it and a second frame, attached by a hinge, was brought down sharply across them to break the fiber. Jonathan's brake exists today in the excellent Pioneer Farm Museum which has been installed in the barn Andrew built across Hale Run from the house.

The men folks then "swingled" the broken pieces with a large wooden knife, or swingle, to get the shives, or pieces of wooden bark, out of the flax. The women took over from there, using a large wooden comb called a hatchel to separate the tow—the coarser part—from the softer flax. "Grandma spun the flax on a little wheel, aunt carded"—or combed—"the tow making flat rolls about a foot long, then spun on big wheel." This equipment is shown, and the process described, in the Farm Museum.

Eveline goes on:

Spinning flax is such pretty work, but I had to learn under difficulties, for when I began to spin grandpa would laugh at me and say there, there, there, in such a funny way until he would make me laugh and the thread would run out of my fingers onto the spool, would have to stop and wind the thread and start again . . . But I persevered and learned to spin flax. After the yarn was spun, was boiled in ashes and water and it was a big job to rinse the ashes out of the yarn, then boiled in clear water . . . The cloth for sheets, pillow cases and table linen was bleached by weting in weak lye, then in clear water, alternately, often as it got dry in the grass.

Because cotton was rare, homespun linen and flannel took its place for men's every-day clothes. Underwear was undoubtedly made of wool. But linen was also used for towels, grain bags, and aprons, "also yarn for stockings and black, brown and white thread" for sewing and mending. Eveline's Aunt Mary "used to spin tow, twisting it very slack for candle wicking. If anyone wanted a good string they would get a ball of tow and someone to twist it, then pull out a string as long as they wanted." Two such strings were pulled out and twisted together.

Sheep were raised in the Valley from the very earliest days, though the bears and wolves were a menace the first four or five years. By Eveline's time the "woolen factories" in Ghent did part of the work of turning wool into cloth. After the sheep were sheared, she recalled, the wool would "lie about two weeks for ticks to die." Then the dirt was picked out, and dead ends clipped off, and some of the wool was "washed with blue", to be mixed later with white wool for use in knitting stockings. Black sheeps' wool was also used to mix with white to make "gray mix". The raw wool was sent to Ghent to be "mixed and carded". Then the women spun it and sent it back to the factory again to be fulled and pressed, ready for making the great coats and jackets Mercy cut and sewed. In the later years the women "usually made pants and vests and hired tailors to cut coats, and some (hired) tailors to make them."

No loom has survived among the relics which have come down to us in the Hale house, because they were too bulky to keep when they were no longer used. But we know that most of the Hale and Hammond women wove, and Elijah's daughter Mary, Eveline's aunt, learned when she was sixteen. "From that time until 1871 (she) done a good deal of different kinds, flannel, table linen, blankets, coverlids, and carpets," as well as the wool and linen for clothes and the like. In her later years this sort of work must have been merely a hobby.

Eveline tells us too that Jason Hammond, Mary's uncle, made the first loom she used. It was "well made. He must have understood something of carpentry, must have been hard work, especially the planing, for it was made of oak. She wove many hundreds of yards with it," and may have done work for all the Hales and Hammonds.

Jonathan and Elijah Hale liked a kind of jacket Eveline calls a "Wamus" to wear for work around the farm. They were made of flannel dyed "madder red, made loose and lined with some of the same, the sleeves (lined) with cotton cloth . . . In 1840 and 50 we used to send white (homespun) flannel to factory in Ghent to have it colored and pressed for winter dresses, and they were nice and comfortable. Grandma loved to knit socks and we also knit mittens to sell and use."

Samplers were made by girls in the early days of the Reserve, and Eveline's mother made one while she attended school in Hudson, which was around 1820. Some of Eveline's treasured possessions at the time she wrote her memoirs were her mother's sampler, needle book, and a table cloth she spun and wove before her marriage.

*   *   *   *   *   *

Food in the Valley was plain, monotonous, but abundant. Most of it was grown on the farm. In Eveline's girlhood the wheat was ground in a mill in Middlebury, the early name for Akron, oats were grown for the live stock, corn served as food for both man and beast. Pork was the most common meat because it could be cured, but beef and mutton were also eaten. And there were chickens, ducks, geese, and turkeys, and of course eggs, butter, and milk. Potatoes were a staple of diet and were probably served boiled or baked, and they and turnips and cabbage were stored in the cellars. Apples and peaches grown on his farm were sold by Jonathan to men like Dr. Hudson of Hammond's Corners in the early twenties. There was a variety of squash and pumpkins and the Indians grew beans, though there is no mention of them in sources like Eveline Cook. No one thought of salads, and tomatoes were not introduced as food for many years. Wild strawberries, raspberries, blueberries and grapes added to the diet for part of the year, and by the thirties or earlier domestic varieties were being grown.

For sweetening in these early years we know that the Jonathan Hales had honey, for the hives are visible in Ruger's drawing. There were also hives in about the same place in Jonathan's grandson's day. But the basic sweetening for the entire Western Reserve before cane sugar arrived in quantity was maple syrup and sugar.

The Indians had a sugar bush near the site of the present attractive one, back from the house at the foot of the hillside where the maple trees grow.

Ancient trees can still be found bearing the faint mark of the V-shaped wedges made by Indian tomahawks to drain the sap. Jonathan bored holes instead.

Eveline says that alder stalks were used for "spiles", the small plugs inserted in the holes to drain the sap. "And to catch the sap they made troughs I think of basswood." Her grandfather Elijah had "what he called a howel, made something like a hammer, head like a hammer only square, the other part (or end) was sharp and slightly rounding to dig out the trough with. Grandma had bread tray made in same way, only finished much nicer, outside and in." The sap was then boiled in big iron kettles to make syrup and boiled again to make sugar. The sap flowed in March and early April, depending on the weather. Though the sugar was dark in the early years by later standards, "I used to think it real good . . . Think our folks made what they need and used all they made," and this was probably true of Jonathan Hale as well, for no maple sugar sales appear in the early account books. In Eveline's childhood cane sugar began to appear in the Valley and she remembers it being used for icing on cakes, and "of being on hand to have plate and knife to scrape."

Jonathan's original sugar camp, on the site of the present charming little Victorian building, was built of logs and resembled on a smaller scale the sugar bushes now used in Geauga County. But small maple sugar operations like that of the Hales were common all over northeastern Ohio and east into Pennsylvania and New York—and also, of course, in Vermont.

"When I was quite young," Eveline writes, "grandpa and uncle"—Elijah and Jonathan Hale, that is—"used to thresh wheat and oats with flails," and they had a fanning mill to separate the grain from the chaff. But in "1834 or 5 had threshing machine," and it must have been one of the first in the Valley.

"From what I can remember of early days," she goes on, "it was through much hard work that corn was raised. They had no cultivator in those days . . . it had all to be done with a hoe."

Oxen were used in Eveline's girlhood for heavier chores like plowing and hauling logs or stone and she often saw her grandfather "yoke up the oxen. He would put the yoke on the off ox, slip the bow around his neck and fasten it, then lift up the other end from the ground with his left hand and take the other bow in right hand and motion to the nigh ox that stood looking on. Then he"—the ox, that is—"would walk up to his mate, yoke was put on his neck and bow fastened."

Eveline mentions a few ways in which corn was cooked and none of them sound very appetizing. One was hulled corn. To prepare it corn was put in a kettle "with some ashes tied up in a cloth and let it boil, till hulls were loose, then skim out in cold water and rub it through two or three waters till only corn was left, then boil in clear water and set away. Would be ate with milk or warmed up with butter and salt, think cream would improve it." There was nothing either quick or easy about cooking in those days! Eveline goes on:

> When I was young grandma cooked hominey corn ground very coarse like cracked corn we now get for young chickens. She used to set it before the fire, but not boiled it, stirred it often and skimmed it. Think she cooked it about three hours. Grandma used to make such pudding. When cold would fry it very nicely, and I know that fried mush with butter and maple sirup is much more to my taste than bone-set tea, and by the way thoroughwort tea was never failing remedy for all ills in our family.

Corn meal was also made into Johnny cake, with milk and eggs added, and then baked. And Eveline recalls a "boiled Indian pudding, made like Johnny cake, boiled three hours, if water boiled out put in hot water, then served with butter, cream and maple sugar, and they are good enough for any-body." They were also baked instead of boiled, she says, and she made them herself "in former years." The difference seems to have been the milk and eggs, and the Johnny cake sounds more tasty.

Still another dish Eveline describes was made from old bread after new bread had been baked. She called it "rusk and milk". The old bread was broken up and set in tins and placed in the oven to dry, then pounded fine with a mortar and eaten with milk. "It was very good," Eveline says of this simple dish. "When Grandpa eat it he wanted it to soak a while first, but would want it in his particular bowl."

Boiling of course was done in iron kettles hung on cranes which swung out over the open fires in the big fireplaces like that in the basement of "Old Brick", and baking was usually done in the small ovens like that to the left of this fireplace, with a place for coals or a fire beneath. Eveline's grandmother also had a useful utensil she called a "baking kettle". It stood on legs about three inches high and you "could put coals under it, had a cover and put coals on it, the edge rolled up to keep them from rolling off. Also a handle, so she could take an iron hook and lift the cover off. Bottom of kettle flat, and same size as top and bottom." She used this until a brick oven was added to the fireplace in the log cabin up the hill. Later Sarah had a tin oven which she apparently placed on a grill on top of the fire.

For years the Hales used home-made wash tubs. "Grandpa or uncle," Jonathan, that is, "got a barrel and sawed it in two in middle, making two. There were no handles of course, so they bored 4 holes on opposite sides to carry them, and when I got old enough to help carry them found they were hard on the fingers, were heavy when empty, made of oak."

"About the same time," Eveline goes on, "they bought or hired made two wash boards, which I think were a new thing to use"—this was around 1835. "Both aunts used them but grandma would not, and no wonder for they were poor things to use. Grandpa wore tow and linen cloths in summer. After he had been logging or burning brush, I don't see how grandma could wash his clothes without a washboard, but she did all those years . . . Our folks saved their ashes," and the Jonathan Hales did too, "made soap in spring . . . In those days we did not have clothes pins nor for many years after. Think they put clothes on line. If they blew off, go up and put them on again, or pin them with common pins."

The Hales had cows, of course, as well as horses, and milk was an important part of their diet. However, by some strange quirk neither Jonathan nor his cousin Elijah knew how to milk, or would learn. O. W. Hale reports that Jonathan, astonishingly, used to bring his cow into Mercy's sick room to be milked. If she was unable to do it, he would lead the poor beast a quarter of a mile to Jason Hammond's house down the road. In emergencies, when the Hammonds couldn't help, he led the cow up the long hill to Elijah's house where one of the women did the job. Yet, as Eveline remarked, Jonathan's fingers were agile enough on the violin.

We know that life was not all work in the brick house and its neighbors. Eveline recalls that the Hales and the Hammonds used to get together on Thanksgiving, Christmas, and New Years. "Surely these were the pleasantest gatherings I ever enjoyed." The big basement room of Jonathan's house must have been the usual meeting place. In summer they gathered for noisy 4th of July celebrations, and the weddings and births in the Hale and Hammond families were frequent cause for parties. Jonathan and Andrew would play the violin and clarinet and everyone else would sing.

Jonathan's violin playing continued as the years went by. Eveline remembers that "Once uncle said to me, 'Don't it look silly for an old man like me to play the fiddle?' I replied, no, indeed. They enjoyed it and so did the others." O. W. Hale recalls that his grandfather in his later years used to stand on the little porch in the summer time and play jigs on the violin for his children and grandchildren.

Jonathan was a good host as well. We have an amusing letter he received from an old friend named D. V. Bradford, apparently an Akron man though the letter was written in Cleveland on January 14, 1839.

> The time to me seems long since I had the pleasure of an old fashioned hearty shake of the hand—& long common chit-chat with my never to be forgotten friend, of the snug *brick palace* located among the

rugged hills of Bath . . . & oft wish I was seated with him before his old kitchen fire, a few good apples—and Mug of good cider—where I could hear him tell a few anecdotes—sing a few tunes.

But the time was growing late for Jonathan Hale. His health and his sight were failing after 1840, and in his remaining years he wore a green eyeshade. In October of 1842 he wrote a letter to his daughter Sophronia Hammond which describes his ailments, and ends on a note one would expect from Jonathan Hale.

"Altho almost blind and having a sick headache too I thought I would try to write a line or two which may be the last. My health and strength I feel to be declining and cannot expect to stay much longer. The Latins would say ("Tempus fugit") time flies, and so let it fly, if we are ready to acquiess in the dispensation of Providence."

IX

THE LATER YEARS
1850 - 1938

The death of Jonathan Hale in 1854 at the age of 77 marked the end of an era in the Valley. For many years he had been the most important citizen in the northeastern corner of Bath and the adjoining parts of Boston. Like his ancestor the "Bully" of Glastonbury, Jonathan was a big man, six feet tall and weighing 180 pounds. A daguerreotype of Jonathan and Sarah, probably taken between 1845 and 1850, shows Jonathan with a large-boned face, unruly hair, and deep-set, penetrating eyes. There is an alertness about this interesting face which the daguerreotypist caught. Sarah looks older and very tired.

O. W. Hale was thirteen at his grandfather's death, and in his sketch of Jonathan's life he recalled that he was a "kindhearted man, and yet very stern in his manner, and I well remember fearing him on account of his appearance." He was ill during most of the years his grandson knew him best and he wore a green eyeshade much of the time. "In government," of his family, that is, "he was very strict and seemed not only to believe but did practice the old Bible doctrine of not sparing the rod . . . He was quite fixed in his religious beliefs and was a man of strong prejudices." This we can well believe.

His methods of raising a family were all too typical of the times, but to fill out the picture we know that Jonathan had an excellent sense of the comic— to General Bierce he was "something of a wag"—and a deep and touching affection for both Mercy and Sarah, as well as his children. His love of music was many-sided and one of them he put to an important use in the Cuyahoga country. He was alert to the times he lived in, probably beyond the evidence we now possess. It is a loss that Eveline Cook, who no doubt was spared the rod, did not tell us more about her uncle, for she obviously saw a side of him his grandsons did not see.

Jonathan's will was written in 1846, proof that his health was failing, and it contained a list of bequests for all of his and Mercy's children, the Mather children, and his own and Sarah's. Some of the bequests to the Mathers and to his and Mercy's younger children are amusing:

> 5th To my Son James Madison Hale I give one hundred dollars including a part which is paid and the remainder to be paid at a reasonable time after my Decease 6th I give to my wife's Son

George Mather one yoke of three year old Steers worth at least $30.00
7 I give to my wife's Daughter Jane [Andrew's wife] the sum of Ten
dollars & a good Cow and further for the good feeling & kindness
manifested to me & her Mother five dollars more to be appropriated
for a gold ring with Suitable device for the occasion.

To his and Sarah's children he was more generous, giving their daughter
Mercy Ann, named after Mercy Piper, of course, $150 "with her clothing,
schooling, and boarding." But Betsey Mather got only $10 and "a Cow of
which she has nearly received but I will give her five dollars more She can
appropriate to what purpose She pleases." What he meant by "nearly received"
is a mystery.

One very interesting bequest was a gift to "my two sons Jonathan Dudley
Hale & Samuel Clark Hale." They were his and Sarah's children who were 15
and eight respectively when their father wrote his will. He gave them "my
large Bible, my books called Panoplist and Missionary Herald allso Jays &
Barders Sermons and all the rest of my Books, unless I write the name to whom
I give it in the title page of the Book."

To Sarah, Jonathan Dudley, and Samuel, Jonathan left a third of his
"farm . . . and the half of my House & Barn" as well as the household goods
and furniture "for their use and benefit."

William received one-third of the north parts of lots 11 and 12, which
included Jonathan's big barn and William's own house across the road, as
well as a third part of lot 13, up the hill.

We are more interested, however, in Andrew's portion, for it was he who
spent the rest of his life on the farm. The will reads: "To my son Andrew
I give the north third part of Lots No. 11-12 & the middle third part of Lot 13,
and the 14 acres in Lot 14 & such share of the House & Barn & ground as
he now occupies." To this, as the years went by, Andrew added by purchase
from the other heirs almost all of the farm Jonathan owned at his death. In
Andrew's own will he lists 274 acres, including 97 in Lot 11, the same in Lot
12—the "northern two thirds" of each—and the eastern half of Lot 13 on the
hill, the part which adjoined his other two lots. The 14 acres in Lot 14,
Jonathan himself sold to Elijah Hale's son Theodore a few weeks after writing
his will.

Sarah Cozad Mather Hale, who had apparently been ill of cancer for many
years, died in 1855, and it was then that Andrew began to add to his farm,
by buying the shares of Jonathan Dudley and Samuel Hale. This also left the
house in Andrew's hands and he needed the space for his growing family.
When Sarah died, Andrew's daughter Pamelia was 16, Sophronia 14, Clarissa
12, and Charles Oviatt only 5. Alida was born that year and Andrew and
Jane's sixth and last child was John Park Hale, born in 1864. To carry the

children's story further, Pamelia married William C. Oviatt and they had no children. Sophronia, like Pamelia named after an aunt, married an aggressive young man named Samuel J. Ritchie and we shall hear more of this interesting couple again. Clarissa married L. H. Ashmun and bore him two children. Charles Oviatt Hale, better known as "C.O.", the oldest of Andrew's two sons, married Pauline Cranz, and their life together in the house and on the farm fills most of the last pages of this story. Alida married Thomas Humphrey and the couple had five children, and Andrew's youngest, John Park Hale, married Zadellia Frank and they had one child.

To repeat a bit from an earlier chapter, Andrew made important changes in the house, to add to its appearance and increase its efficiency as a place to live. First, he moved the south wing he had built for his family around to the rear, attaching it more conveniently to the living room his father had added. Parallel this he built another wing to the north, which provided space for storing food and coal. It had a "corn room" on the second floor which still shows its original beams and flooring. Either Andrew or his son and heir, "C. O.", remodelled the rear part of this wing and opened an outside door, renting the room to the guests we will hear more about later. The wing was also connected with the old living room by a porch, which has since been enlarged and is now used as an office. The exteriors of these buildings were originally clapboard, but in recent years they have been faced with brick to match the rest of the house.

Before his death, Jonathan had built a big, unpainted barn which still stands across the road and has long since been painted red. Its original silo has been torn down. In 1866 Andrew built the slate-roofed barn behind the house and across Hale Run which now houses the Pioneer Farm Museum. During his life and part of C.O.'s, it was used for sheep which grazed the park-like woodlands up the slope toward the old lime field. Later C. O. made it into a dairy barn. Andrew also built a carriage house that stood by the road and has now been moved west of the parking lot.

*   *   *   *   *   *

It is clear that Jonathan's health required the help of Andrew in running the farm as early as 1844, ten years before his death, for Andrew kept an account book which has come down to us covering the years from 1844 to 1850. While Andrew shouldered most of the work, with the help of a number of hired men, and kept the records which Jonathan was barely able to read, one can be sure that the strong-willed Jonathan gave plenty of sound advice to his very much milder but capable son. In spite of it, we can be sure that in these years it was actually Andrew's farm, and one that he loved.

The account book has much to tell. Briefly, a far more varied list of items was bought or sold than in the accounts of the early years. Barter was still a factor, but coin or bills were clearly the principal means of exchange. In the typical pages, it appears that the final reckoning for an account off balance, as most of them were, was usually made with cash.

The old basic crops were still there—potatoes, wheat, corn, pork, beef, apples, and flour. But by 1844 Andrew was beginning to grow and sell a few of these crops and a number of new ones in amounts far larger than his father. He was not selling a mere surplus of the food he required around the farm, but growing in considerable quantity a selected few items for the market. Perhaps the most important of these was pork, with its by-products tallow and soap, or "soap grease". Another, and one which became a basic item in the years to come, was sheep. Andrew sold mutton as well as wool but no lamb is mentioned in the accounts. Apples also appear in considerable quantity, and these became a specialty of the place. Something which must have been Jonathan's idea was onions, which Andrew sold by the bushel. There are entries for 8 pounds of cheese at 10 cents, 17 pounds of honey from the hives which date back to the days of the cabin, at $2.12. Vinegar was sold by the gallon, but there is no mention of cider. In smaller amounts Andrew sold turnips, lard, beeswax, beans, and butter. Oddly, no maple sugar or syrup is listed at all, in the accounts of 1844-1850.

Eveline, in her inimitable style, says that Andrew kept three cows, and unlike his father, his uncle Elijah, and his son C. O., he was able to milk them. He would "stand with a pail in one hand and milking stool in the other, would say 'come Speck', or 'come Nubbin' or 'Nuppet', can't remember which, and the cow he called would come to him. Then he would look so pleased about it. They knew their names, for the ones he didn't call would stand still chewing their cuds." Eveline had a talent for putting flesh and blood into the sober entries of the old account books.

Andrew hired far more help around the farm than Jonathan or his father had ever done in Glastonbury or Bath, but his wages were low. He paid Orlando Mack $1.50 for three days' chopping wood, where Jonathan would probably have paid $3.00. This was unusually low even for Andrew, but his normal wage scale was not much higher. As a rule he paid 75 cents a day for cutting corn or threshing, 63 cents for hoeing, 60 cents for butchering, and his top was $1 a day for "sheareing" sheep. Horse-shoeing is mentioned more frequently in these accounts, and Andrew paid from a quarter to a dollar for jobs, depending of course on what was done. An interesting item is dated 1847, when he paid Mr. Jackson, the blacksmith, 20 cents for "making a bolt for a cultivator." Times were changing indeed.

We have some scraps of Andrew's later account books, from the 1860s, and they show no important change in his farming and crops. This of course was after the death of his father when he was entirely on his own. However, in the 1870s he turned his attention increasingly to the growing of apples, and we have the plans he drew for setting out a small new orchard. His son, C. O., carried this interest much farther.

Andrew, as we know, inherited his father's love of singing, played the clarinet and probably the violin. There was a Handel Society in Hudson in the 1840s and Andrew may have been a member, for Eveline tells us that he taught a singing school there, "and it seems very safe to conclude that he did in Bath." This seems to mean that a singing school and a choir were not at all identical, and that the school was devoted to more secular music, no doubt for young ladies.

But the choir in the little Congregational Church in Bath, built as we know in 1833 and which he served for years as Secretary, was Andrew's greatest love. The choir had 12 members, Eveline recalls, including herself, William, three of the Hammonds from around the Corners, and Andrew, its leader. Eveline sang in this choir from 1840 until 1852, and

> during these 12 years I don't remember one Sabbath going to church and Uncle Andrew *not* there to lead the singing. How long before, and how long after these dates he was choirmaster do not know. He led the singing too with life and energy, dependent upon no instrument to get the right key but his faithful tuning fork. I think great credit is due him and Cousin William in singing and in many other things in maintaining church services for many years. They were not gentlemen of leisure, but hardworking farmers living 4 miles from church, Cousin Andrew took great pleasure in having his children learn to sing and in singing with them.

The most important change in the life of the Valley which took place during Andrew's later years was the construction of the Valley Railroad. It was a project dear to the hearts of Cleveland businessmen because it would bring to the city coal from the new fields near Massillon. The old Mahoning fields were about exhausted and the great mines in Western Pennsylvania and West Virginia were too far away in these years for cheap transportation. Coal was shipped by the Canal, but a railroad could handle far more at a better price.

Committees were formed in Cleveland in the late 1860s to sell bonds and obtain from the State part of the canal bed in the flats as a terminus for the road. Councilman John Huntington, later a founder of the Museum of Art, was a leader in the matter and he had the help of his friends Nathan Payne, J. H. Wade and City Treasurer Sylvester T. Everett, for whom the little crossroads at Unionville was eventually renamed.

Construction of the railroad began in 1873 but was halted by the great panic which struck that year, and the winding single-track line was not opened until 1880. Its broad-eaved little freight and passenger stations, painted red, brought a minor prosperity to towns in the Valley, notably Peninsula, a late-comer among them. There were stations at Everett, Ira, and Botzum, near the Hales, and that at Ira—named for Ira Watkins—was the most convenient. It provided the Valley people with faster transportation to Akron as that city began to grow after the Civil War, and to Cleveland, but the Hales continued to ship a few items like straw and cordwood by the old canal, which still carried coal from Massillon. The railroad and the canal competed for local freight, and partly because of this the road was never financially successful, going bankrupt in 1894. The Baltimore & Ohio bought an interest to keep it alive and purchased the entire road in 1915.

Today an occasional diesel pounds through the Valley and the line serves the B & O as a link between Cleveland and its main line which passes through Akron. But in recent years trucks and autos and busses have taken over the freight and passenger traffic and the little stations have disappeared.

In his later years Andrew suffered a number of painful ailments, variously diagnosed as boils or neuralgia. Operations failed to help him and there seems to have been at least a possibility that his affliction was cancer, for the pain was unbearable. He made an attempt to shoot himself but this was thwarted by members of his family. After a second attempt which wounded him severely, he died on July 30, 1884. Like all the Hales he was outspoken in his opinions, though certainly milder than his father. But "in its broadest sense," a biographer writes, "he was strictly an honest man." His wife and step-sister, Jane Mather Hale, lived on for twenty years, occupying the first floor bedroom which had once been Jonathan's.

*　*　*　*　*　*

In his will, Andrew again divided the land of the Hales, but in a far simpler way than Jonathan. He gave to his older son, Charles Oviatt, known to all his friends as "C. O.", the house and the surrounding 97 acres which made up the northern two-thirds of Lot 11. To his younger son, John Park, he gave outright the 80 acres in Lot 13 on top of the hill as well as an un-divided interest which he shared with his brother in the northern two-thirds of Lot 12. Andrew's four daughters were each given $1,000, minus the amounts they had received in advance. His nephew, Othello W. Hale, the family his-torian and William's son, was made executor.

Undivided interests in farm land are likely to be unsatisfactory to all concerned, and in 1888 C. O. bought from John his share in Lot 12. Later John disposed of his half of Lot 13 and it passed out of the family. This left C. O. with a compact plot of 194 acres made up of the northern two-thirds of Lots 11 and 12. They had always been the heart of the farm, and in a sense were the farm of 150 acres which Jonathan had written about to Mercy back in 1810.

C. O. had been born in the house in 1850 and he received a better formal education than any of his branch of the Hale family before him. He went to a school in Richfield, then briefly to Western Reserve College in Hudson, and from there to Oberlin, where he graduated in 1870. Because of this rather scattered education, his tastes were a good deal more sophisticated than those of his father. He farmed out the routine chores of the place, pursuing instead a few horticultural hobbies with considerable success and profit, and turned the house and its lovely grounds into a show-place of the Valley. It became a favorite vacation spot for dozens of socially prominent Cleveland and Akron families for some forty years. The gay comings and goings and the delightful confusion about the place would have bewildered his grandfather Jonathan.

C. O. also took more interest in local public affairs than any of the other Hales before him. He was a trustee of the Township for three years, and, more important, he was elected to the Ohio House of Representatives as a Republican. He served two consecutive terms of two years each, beginning in 1892 and a third in 1914. He loved to talk about his career in Columbus, particularly in promoting the welfare of the public schools and their teachers.

In 1875 C. O. married Pauline Cranz. Her parents were William T. and Mary Drushal Cranz who had come to the Valley from Holmes County and bought the old house Jason Hammond had built in 1818. Pauline was teaching school at the time of her marriage. The ties between the Cranz and the Hale families, and the brick house and the land around it, have been intimate ever since. The Cranzes own part of the Hammond land today and some to the north in Lot 10 where Aaron Miller settled.

Pauline's nephew, Carl Cranz, was for eighteen years one of the tenants who took over the farming of the place for C. O. He now lives in an attractive house on top of the hill on Ira Road with a magnificent view of the Valley. He owns land there which was part of Jonathan's purchase from Thomas Bull. Another nephew, Harmon Cranz, now lives in the old Hammond house, which has been considerably enlarged. Both men have supplied invaluable information about the house, the life that was lived there, and the farming which was done on the place.

It was Andrew who began to use the brick house for "genteel paying guests," in the early 1870s. But C. O. developed this aspect much further and made it his principal interest. The farming and the upkeep of the grounds around the house he left to tenant farmers like Carl Cranz, who paid him partly in cash and partly in supplies for the table. He had a few horticultural hobbies which he pursued on the place, as we shall see, but his principal income was derived from the tenant farmers and the guests. "Hale Inn", as it was sometimes called in later years, was probably best known as a summering place between 1880 and World War I, and for the last part of this period a few guest books have survived which give us amusing notes on the activities there as well as the names of some of the guests. C. O. served as the host and became known as "The Squire."

Most of the guests who came for a week or so with their families, or even for an entire summer, were Clevelanders. Akron people usually came out for the day or overnight. Meals were cooked and served in the south wing of the house by Pauline and girls from school or college. In the summer the guests dined in the big back room around an enormous table, and in other seasons in a smaller room just off the living room, which had been added in Jonathan's time. There was a pantry at one side of the wing and cooking was done on a stove which was laboriously moved to the adjoining north wing in summer and back into the south wing at other times of year. This sort of casual arrangement was typical of the place and part of its charm.

Guests were lodged in the bedrooms of the old brick house, and in busy seasons C. O. and Pauline gave up their own room there and slept under the beams in the corn room above the north wing. As we have seen, there was a small bedroom at the end of this wing on the ground floor which had a private door of its own. The rest of the wing was used to store coal and other supplies. There was no modern plumbing in any part of the house until very recent times and two privies stood at the rear of the house. Ever since the house was built, and perhaps before, water had been drawn by a bucket from a spring in the front yard. It was covered with a large tile which was raised by a handle and today it is capped with a concrete block. The pump beside the porch at the rear of the old house was more convenient by far and was installed by C. O.

The P. H. Fry family from Cleveland built a one-room cottage northwest of the house, at the end of the garden we shall describe in a moment. It was used by other families as well. Up on the park-like hillside there were scattered clearings, and other cottages were built there by men like William Higgins of East Ohio Gas and his friend Howard Jones of Standard Oil who also kept riding horses on the place. Around 1910 the W. L. Kyle family of Akron built the only cottage which survives, across Hale Run from the house. The second floor of the carriage barn was used as a bunk house shared by male guests and the men who worked on the place.

Whole families boarded there and so did groups of school and university people. Some of them came for a few days or weeks and a few spent the summer. Literally hundreds of people came and went during these years and those who are now alive remember the place with delight and affection. Among them, beginning in the 1870s and continuing for years, were George W. Bierce and his mother. Mr. Bierce has been of assistance in assembling the furniture and other material now in the house, a good deal of which was there when he used to visit the place. As many of the rooms as possible he has restored as he used to know them.

Others from Cleveland whose names appear in the guest book were the Rev. Dr. William W. Bustard and his family of Euclid Avenue Baptist Church, known as the "Rockefeller Church" from its most famous and generous member; Dean Charles D. Williams of Trinity Cathedral, and Rabbi Moses Gries of The Temple. W. T. Holliday, for many years president of Standard Oil of Ohio, Victor Morgan, general manager of The Cleveland Press, and Judge Arthur Day were other Cleveland guests.

Among those who came for briefer visits were Mrs. Solon L. Severance, her daughter Mrs. B. L. Millikin and her husband, Dr. Millikin, and Malcom Vilas. A number of the Cozads from the vicinity of University Circle came for visits, as well as Mathers and Hales. Akron guests who came for a day or overnight included Frank Seiberling and his family, the Arthur Saalfield family, and the Albert J. Hoovers, and these guests are only a few.

It was a favorite place to bring the children, and their comments written in the guest books show what they did there. Like their elders, they played croquet, roamed over the farm, and watched the chickens and farm animals. One little boy wrote, "I threw water on Elsie." Comments by adults call the house an "ideal place" or exclaim, "Oh, what bliss!" Judge J. A. Kohler of Akron "got up early," no doubt to roam the fields and woodlands before breakfast.

On one occasion a "Tally-Ho Party" stopped off from Akron and all of its fifteen or twenty members signed the book. This was in 1902, and a couple of years later they were back with a few automobiles puffing along behind the big tally-hos and their horses.

One child who loved the place was Frank N. Wilcox, who is now one of Cleveland's most distinguished artists and until recently a member of the faculty of the Institute of Art. He visited the Hale place in the summer of 1902 and recalls the stories "The Squire" told of the Indians who used to live on the hill across the road. This inspired him to model a small figure of an Indian chief, probably from the clay Jonathan had used for making brick, and C. O. placed it on a mantelpiece in the old house.

It was a house with an informal charm all its own, and if there were occasional inconveniences, they were part of the fun. It was a relaxing place in a lovely setting of gardens, hedges, fruit trees, open meadow and farm land, framed by the forested hills. But it seems clear that the engaging personalities of the Squire and his wife, Pauline, had the most to do with its popularity.

The grounds around the old brick house and its barns and outhouses were far more elaborately planted in C. O.'s time, and Andrew's too, than they are today. On the south side of the lawn toward the Run was a tall, clipped hedge, and around the southern side of the house was a variety of closely trimmed trees and shrubs, all of it known at the time as topiary effects. Two great trees which have since been cut down stood on the lawn near the road and the Run, and apples and lilacs lined the north side of the drive leading up to the house.

There was a big garden approximately on the site of the present parking lot, with a tall border of flowers on the side toward the drive. At the eastern end of the garden there was a row of 35 beehives, an inheritance from the days of the cabin and a special hobby of Jonathan's grandson. To the north beyond the garden was a small apple orchard with an octagonal chicken house in the middle for another of the Squire's hobbies, the Black Spanish chickens which were unique in the Valley. North of the orchard and the chicken house, where the ground dips down, was a "secondary garden", more for use in the kitchen than for show. Beyond this was a fence and pasture land which swept away up the gentle slope to Lot 10 and the boundary of C. O.'s land. West of the more formal garden, near the cottage built by the Cobbs, were an ice house and smoke house for preserving and curing meat.

C. O.'s principal hobby was growing apples, and he had about 110 varieties on the place. He was a charter member of the Summit County Horticultural Society and remained active in it for 54 years. His apples were a regular feature of the Society's shows in Akron. They were not planted in one or two large orchards, but scattered about the farm and its gardens in rows and attractive small plantings. Besides those we have mentioned on either side of the garden, there was a double row along the road leading back to the sugar house—though the ones there now are of recent planting. In the spring the blossoms were a lovely sight and the fruit and cider were major attractions of the place. In the fall of 1902 the guest book contains the eloquent comment written by an over-night visitor: "Apples, apples, apples!"

The Squire also made a hobby of the old sugar bush, which he rebuilt in the picturesque Victorian style we see today. It had a chimney in C. O.'s time and the vents in the little tower were used for escaping steam and to cool the place. None of the equipment he used has come down to us, but his kettles, buckets, and spiles were far more modern than anything Jonathan ever knew.

Groups of school children from Akron and even Cleveland used to come to the place in early spring for sugar parties, and Carl Cranz remembers meeting them at Ira Station with a wagon. C. O. charged a nominal fee and supplied the meals, and the children scrambled about in the woods and helped empty the buckets and carry the sap to the sugar house. Naturally, they bought syrup and sugar to take home, as did other guests throughout the year.

C. O. had about twenty acres devoted mainly to sugar maples on the hillsides along Hale Run, and Carl Cranz has counted ninety trees in the woods adjoining his own property along Ira Road. In a good year these trees produced as much as 300 gallons of syrup. In the fall there were "nutting parties" for children, run on a similar plan, with chestnuts the principal crop. Prominent Clevelanders remember going down to the place by the railroad for these outings when they were young. One reason C. O. and Pauline welcomed these young people so warmly was that they had no children of their own.

Both Andrew and C. O., and perhaps Jonathan too, sold timber on the place, and one of the men who cut it in Andrew's later years was an aggressive, competent young man named Samuel J. Ritchie. He was born in the township in 1838 and attended Western Reserve College for a year at the age of eighteen. For a living he turned to the lumbering business, and one of his operations was cutting the timber on the northern slope of Andrew Hale's land. A ravine which slashes down the hillside is still called Ritchie Gull. Samuel also owned boats on the Ohio Canal in which he shipped lumber to market, and some was used to build the first Akron hospital. More important for the story of the farm, in 1865 Samuel married Andrew's daughter Sophronia. The couple settled in Tallmadge and they had three children—Lewis Andrew, Clara Belle, and Charles Edward, who was known as Ned.

Ritchie's active mind took him into a variety of business interests, including the production of sewer pipe and the purchase of West Virginia coal and timber lands. Far more important was his interest in iron mines in Hastings County in central Ontario Province. To bring his ore to the lake port of Trenton he built the Central Ontario Railroad in 1882 and became its president. However, the markets for ore in the United States were too remote and the railroad ran into trouble. In the emergency Ritchie turned to the undeveloped copper mines around Sudbury in Northern Ontario to feed his road, organizing in 1886 the Canadian Copper Company of which he also became president.

In the Sudbury country Ritchie bought claims for important copper lands and to secure a smelter to handle the ore he shipped on his railroad, he formed an alliance with Robert M. Thompson, a Canadian engineer who had a copper mine in Orford, Quebec, and a plant in Bayonne, New Jersey. But the Bayonne furnace had trouble with the Sudbury ore because of its large percentage of nickel, an old complaint in the copper industry. Ritchie turned to the nickel itself to solve his problem, in the form of nickel steel. With the support of influential Canadians, he toured Europe looking for buyers. But thanks to tests made by a Glasgow metallurgist in 1889, he was able to convince the United States Navy of the effectiveness of nickel in hardening its armor plate.

As the use of nickel and nickel steels spread in the navies of the world and in other fields as well, a better corporate structure was obviously needed for the related Canadian firms which were mining and smelting it. As a result, in 1902 the Canadian Copper Company and Thompson's interests in Orford and Bayonne were merged to form the International Nickel Company.

That Ritchie accumulated a sizable fortune in the 1880s and early 1890s there is no doubt, but his disappointments with iron mines in Hastings and his later troubles with copper and nickel caused him heavy losses. During the financial panic of 1893 he was said to have been virtually wiped out, but he recovered and built another large fortune. In 1905 he began the construction of a famous Akron house—for Summit County was always his home—a thirty-room yellow brick mansion at the corner of West Market and Portage Path. A few of its furnishings are now in the Hale House in the Valley.

Samuel Ritchie died suddenly in Charleston, West Virginia, in 1908 while on business concerning his lands in that part of the country. He was a man of restless energy, stubborn hopes, and a talent for business and promotion. Because of his long and frequent absences from Tallmadge and Akron, Sophronia and Clara Belle lived alone pretty much of the time. It was perhaps because of these close ties with her mother that Clara Belle never married. But she learned from her father a great deal about business affairs, and after his death she took over and further developed her own and her mother's share in the estate, living on in the big West Market Street house.

But Clara Belle had other interests as well. Her brother Ned Ritchie had taken an important and intelligent interest in restoring such historical buildings as the Tallmadge Church which Colonel Lemuel Porter had built. He became president of the Summit County Historical Society and contributed generously to the restoration of the Simon Perkins Mansion in Akron which houses the Society, and the John Brown house next door.

It was largely this interest which led Clara Belle and Ned to buy the farm and the old brick house which had been the home of the Hales from the heirs of C. O. after his death, in 1938, at the fine old age of 88.

Clara Belle Ritchie, especially, took a personal interest in the house and its grounds and for a time it seems that she thought of living there. For this and other good reasons she made a number of important repairs which had long been needed. The old bricks Jonathan made had been crumbling away for years and some were crudely patched over with plaster. She replaced them with modern bricks as much like the old as possible, and the only exterior brick from Jonathan's time which remains is on the rear of the original house above the living room. As we have seen, there are more in the walls of the old storage room off the basement.

The basement itself had been used for storage in C. O.'s time and had fallen into disrepair. Miss Ritchie replaced the old stone floor and rebuilt the mantel and baking oven, keeping the woodwork which goes back to Jonathan's day. To add to the beauty of the place, she planted the handsome growth of evergreens on the slope of the ridge across the road. However, she did not farm the land and she never made it her home, living in the big yellow brick house in Akron until her death in 1956.

Miss Ritchie had drawn and signed her will on April 6, 1953, and for the history of the Western Reserve it is important. In brief, it placed the great bulk of her estate in trust for the equal benefit of the City Hospital of Akron— for which her father had cut timber in Ritchie's Gull and maintained an interest all his life—and the Western Reserve Historical Society in Cleveland. Her remarks in respect to the Society's bequest are significant:

> Since my family took a prominent part in the settlement and development of the Western Reserve, it is my desire to perpetuate the history and culture of the Western Reserve. I accordingly direct that the Trustees and the Society take the necessary steps to establish the Hale Farm and the buildings thereon as a museum for the display of books, paintings, furniture, household goods, farm and household implements, china, silver, plate, ornaments, and similar objects, belonging to the period and culture of the Western Reserve. Said Hale Farm when so established as a museum shall be open to public inspection and display to the end that the greatest number of persons may be informed as to the history and culture of the Western Reserve.

The trustees were also given the power to "erect suitable buildings and make other improvements." With this in mind, the Pioneer Farm Museum was opened in the fall of 1960 in the barn which Andrew built for his sheep. Other additions to the displays on the farm recreating the early life of the Valley are being planned to carry out Miss Ritchie's wishes.

Thus the Hale Farm, as Clara Belle Ritchie herself has named it, will become a monument to Jonathan Hale and his times. For it is the period covered by his life in the Valley, and that of Andrew his son, that is thought of today as the years of the Western Reserve. To later generations the awareness of living within the Reserve, and even its meaning, grew dimmer, as migrants poured into the region who had never heard of its past or the inheritance upon which so much has been built. But today the history and significance of the old Western Reserve of Connecticut are arousing new interest among the descendants of the early settlers and the hundreds of thousands of people who have come to the Reserve from the other states of the Union and the far countries of the world.

NOTES ON SOURCE MATERIAL

All the major sources used in writing this book are mentioned in the text as the story moves along, and they are listed in the Bibliography which follows. But in lieu of footnotes, some comment is required on each chapter as a guide for readers who might be interested in checking the sources. This is particularly true in regard to the manuscript material and the invaluable assistance the author has received from a number of friendly and patient people.

A special debt is owed to Mrs. Frank S. Lally of Daytona Beach, Florida, a great-great-granddaughter of Jonathan Hale. At a most opportune moment she brought to our attention an extremely important collection of Hale family papers to add to those we already had in the Library of the Western Reserve Historical Society. It is impossible to itemize her collection here, but it includes the large majority of the correspondence, accounts, music and other books relating to Jonathan Hale and his family which we have quoted. An outstanding exception which should be noted is the memoir of Eveline Bosworth Cook, which came from another source.

CHAPTER I: THE CUYAHOGA COUNTRY

Most of the material is found in the Bibliography under the headings "The Western Reserve" and "The Portage". Goodspeed's chapters in Perrin's Summit County history are reliable for the Indians in the Valley. Lewis' map of 1755 is published in Baldwin's *Early Maps of Ohio and the West*. General Bierce's amusing but inaccurate work has been used with care, mainly for its local color.

CHAPTER II: THOMAS BULL AND THE WESTERN RESERVE

This chapter is based almost entirely on the rich manuscript material in the Library of the Historical Society. Most of it is listed in the Bibliography under the heading "Connecticut Land Company." The Turhand Kirtland Papers supplied the Bull and Williams correspondence. The text of the drafts, of which there are many other copies, came from the Erie Company Records in the enormous collection of the Simon Perkins Papers. The report of the Classing Committee of 1807 is from the Connecticut Land Company Papers, Volume 17. Tappan's accounts of the Treaty of Fort Industry and his surveys are both from his manuscript *History of the Surveys of the Land West of the Cuyahoga River*. Rial MacArthur's survey notes are entered in the Society's manuscript catalog under "Bath Township, Ohio". Sherman's *Original Ohio Land Subdivisions* was invaluable.

CHAPTER III: THE HALES OF GLASTONBURY

In general refer to "The Hale Family" and "Connecticut" in the Bibliography. Material on the history of the town comes from Chapin. Most of the Hale genealogy is from Jacobus, with some help from O. W. Hale's manuscript with its biographies and genealogy of the Hales. The latter is in the Hale Family Papers. The account books and correspondence are in the same collection. The Hammond material is from that family's genealogy. The deed from Jonathan Hale to Samuel Welles was supplied from the Glastonbury Town Records by Mr. Herbert T. Clark of South Glastonbury and his help is gratefully acknowledged. The author is particularly indebted to Mrs. John T. Blair of Glastonbury who made me welcome in the old house on Main Street in which Jonathan was born.

CHAPTER IV: THE JOURNEY WEST

This chapter is based of course on Jonathan's diary. The original is now in the Hale Family Papers. Most of the other sources are listed under the bibliographical heading "Highways and Travel."

CHAPTER V: THE DIFFICULT MONTHS

The correspondence and account books in the Hale Family Papers are the main source, with additional material, as mentioned in the text, from the Portage County records in Ravenna, the Hammond genealogy, and Goodspeed.

CHAPTER VI: SETTLING THE VALLEY

The correspondence, account books, and hymn books all come as usual from the Hale Papers. Some background material is taken from Goodspeed's chapters on Bath and Boston in Perrin's history. Sources for the War of 1812 will be found in the bibliography under "The Western Reserve" and "The Portage". *The Trump of Fame* is on file in the newspaper collection of the Historical Society. Ruger's lithograph of the cabin hangs in the Hale House in Bath and is also available in the Library of the Historical Society. The one dated about 1880 is in the Hale Family Papers.

CHAPTER VII: BUILDING 'OLD BRICK'

The facts about Middle College are from the minutes of the Trustees of Western Reserve College. The Bosworth genealogy supplied the information on John Bosworth, other than that from his daughter's memoirs. I. T. Frary's well-known book on the early homes of Ohio was helpful. But I am far more in debt to Mrs. Nancy Coe Wixom of the Cleveland Museum of Art, who introduced me to the Hynton house and whose knowledge of domestic architecture in the Western Reserve was invaluable. With Mrs. Wixom and Mr. Carl Cranz, who farmed the place for eighteen years in the days of his uncle C. O. Hale, I have gone over the Hale House almost brick-by-brick and beam-by-beam. Mr. James Waring of the faculty of Western Reserve Academy in Hudson supplied me with facts about Colonel Lemuel Porter and he has been helpful and encouraging in other ways. However, the rather theoretical connection made in this chapter between the three houses is my own, and I assume responsibility.

CHAPTER VIII: LIFE IN THE VALLEY

The sources for the section on the Ohio Canal are given in the Bibliography under that heading. The records of the Bath Church, the children's books, correspondence, and verse are all in the Hale Family Papers. O. W. Hale supplied most of the information about Sarah Cozad Mather Hale, with help from Post's book on Doan's Corners. There is a copy of Eveline Bosworth Cook's memoirs at the Hale House and also in the Historical Society Library.

CHAPTER IX: THE LATER YEARS

Andrew Hale's account book, of course, is in the family papers, and so are an obituary and other biographical material referring to C. O. Hale. But Carl Cranz provided the most useful material about C. O., his recollections of the genial days when the house and farm were known as Hale Inn. I have tramped the fields and woodlands with him and he has patiently described the gardens, orchards, topiary effects, lime field, Indian camp sites, and the old sugar bush he knew so well. However, he is in no way to blame for errors that may appear in this part of the story. I have also talked with many of the men and women who still remember the place, notably Mr. George W. Bierce and Mr. Frank N. Wilcox of Cleveland, and I am grateful for the time and information all of them gave me.

The sketch of the life of Samuel J. Ritchie came from biographical material in his papers, which are in the possession of the Historical Society, and publications of The International Nickel Company filed in the Library, especially the brief pamphlet *The Romance of Nickel,* New York, Revised edition, 1957.

BIBLIOGRAPHY

This is by no means a complete bibliography of the published works on the Western Reserve or Summit County, and certainly not of the vast amount of manuscript material, most of it in the Library of the Western Reserve Historical Society. It is merely a list of the books, manuscripts, maps, and other sources which were of specific help in writing this little book. It is designed as a guide for anyone wanting to examine these sources or do further research on the Hales, the Valley, or Bath Township. For convenience the material is arranged rather generally by subject. The abbreviation "WRHS" is used throughout for Western Reserve Historical Society, in Cleveland, whose library was also the rich source of almost all the books and other material I have mentioned.

THE HALE FAMILY

Cook, Eveline Bosworth, *Recollections . . . relating to the Hale-Hammond Pioneers of Bath, Ohio . . .* (typescript) Akron, 1905

Clark, Mary Bosworth, *Bosworth Genealogy,* Part VI, San Francisco, 1940

Deeds, Hale and Hammond Families, 1810 - 1851, Office of the Recorder, Summit County, Akron, Ohio

Hale Family Papers, Manuscript Collections, WRHS

Hammond, Frederick Stam, *History and Genealogy of the Hammond Families in America,* Vol. 2, Oneida, 1904

Jacobus, Donald Lines, and Waterman, Edgar Francis, *Hale, House and Related Families,* Connecticut Historical Society, Hartford, 1952

Samuel J. Ritchie Papers, Manuscript Collections, WRHS

Town Records, Glastonbury, Conn.

THE WESTERN RESERVE

Badger, Reverend Joseph, *A Memoir of the Rev. Joseph Badger, Containing an Autobiography and Selections from his Private Journal and Correspondence,* Hudson, Ohio, 1851.

Baldwin, Charles Candee, *Early Maps of Ohio and the West,* WRHS Tract No. 25, April, 1875

Benton, Elmer J., *Northern Ohio in the War of 1812,* WRHS Tract No. 92, September, 1913

Bierce, General Lucius Verus, *Historical Reminiscences of Summit County,* Akron, 1854

History of Portage County, Ohio, Warner Beers & Co., Chicago, 1885

Census of the United States, 1820, 1830 (Bath, Boston, Richfield, and North-ampton Townships) Microfilm, WRHS.

Doyle, William B., ed., *Centennial History of Summit County,* Chicago, 1908

Frary, Ihna Thayer, *Early Homes of Ohio,* Richmond, 1934
———— "Old Western Reserve College", *Architectural Record,* December, 1918

George, Milton C., *The Settlement of the Connecticut Western Reserve of Ohio, 1796 - 1850* (typescript), Ann Arbor, 1950

Grismer, Karl H., *Akron and Summit County,* Akron, 1953

Hatcher, Harlan Henthorne, *The Western Reserve,* Indianapolis, 1949

Heckewelder, John, *Map and Description of Northeastern Ohio, 1796,* WRHS Tract No. 64, 1884

Howe, Henry, *Historical Collections of Ohio,* 3 vols., bound in 2, Columbus, 1890

Kilbourn, John, ed., *Ohio Gazetteer,* 6th edition, Columbus, 1819

Knabenshue, Samuel S., "Indian Land Sessions in Ohio", *Ohio Archaeological and Historical Society Publications,* vol. 11, Columbus, 1903

Lane, Samuel A., *Fifty Years and Over of Akron and Summit County,* Akron, 1892

Mahoning Valley Historical Society, *Historical Collections of the Mahoning Valley,* Vol. 1, Youngstown, 1876

Perrin, William Henry, ed., *History of Summit County,* Chicago, 1881

Peters, William E., *Ohio Lands and Their Subdivision,* 2nd edition, Athens and Columbus, 1918

Portage County, Ohio, *Minutes of the County Commissioners,* 1810, Ravenna, Ohio

Porter, William Harvey, *Musical Development of the Western Reserve, Part I, 1803 - 1865* (Typescript) Thesis, Western Reserve University, 1946

Post, Charles Asa, *Doan's Corners and the City Four Miles West,* Cleveland, 1930

Upton, Harriet Taylor, *History of the Western Reserve,* 3 vols., Chicago and New York, 1910

Villard, Oswald Garrison, *John Brown,* Boston, 1910

Waite, Frederick Clayton, *Western Reserve University, the Hudson Era,* Cleveland, 1943

Western Reserve College, *Records of the Trustees . . . from March 1, 1826 to August 28, 1834* (Typescript copy in Freiberger Library, Western Reserve University, original in Treasurer's Office)

Whittlesey, Charles, *Early History of Cleveland,* Cleveland, 1867

Wing, George C., ed., *Early Years of the Western Reserve, with Extracts from the Letters of Ephraim Brown's Family, 1805 - 1845,* Cleveland, 1916

THE PORTAGE

Barnholth, William I., *The Cuyahoga-Tuscarawas Portage, a Documentary History* (typescript), Akron, 1954

Blower, Arthur H., *The Shipyard in Old Portage*, Akron, 1942

Cherry, P. P., *The Portage Path*, Akron, 1921

―――― *The Western Reserve and Early Ohio*, Akron, 1921

Diefenbach, Josephine, *Elijah Wadsworth and the Camp at Old Portage*, (typescript) (Akron) 1935

Smith, James, *An Account of the Remarkable Occurrences in the Life and Travels of Colonel James Smith during his Captivity with the Indians . . . 1755 - 59*, Ohio Valley Historical Series No. 5, Cincinnati, 1870

Whittlesey, Charles, *General Wadsworth's Division, War of 1812*, WRHS Tract No. 5

CONNECTICUT

Adams, James Truslow, *New England in the Republic, 1776 - 1850*, Boston, 1926

―――― *Revolutionary New England, 1691 - 1776*, Boston, 1923

Andrews, Frank DeWitte, *Business Men of the City of Hartford in the Year 1799*, Vineland, N. J., 1909

Chapin, Reverend Alonzo B., *Glastenbury for 200 Years; a Centennial Discourse*, Hartford, 1853

Paullen, Charles O., ed. *Atlas of the Historical Geography of the United States*, Washington, 1932 (Plate 41-D, Wethersfield)

Pope, Virginia B., and Todd, Mary Louise B., *Descendants of Captain Thomas Bull*, Wilmett, Ill., 1939

Rosenberg, Lois Kimball Mathews, *Migration from Connecticut Prior to 1800*, New Haven, 1934

Zeichner, Oscar, Connecticut: *Years of Controversy, 1750 - 1776*, Chapel Hill, 1949

CONNECTICUT LAND COMPANY

Connecticut Land Company Papers, Manuscript Collections, WRHS

Turhand Kirtland Papers, Manuscript Collections, WRHS

MacArthur, Rial, and Warden, R., *A List of the Exterior and Interior Descriptions of Township 3—12th Range . . .* (copy) Manuscript Collections, WRHS

Simon Perkins Papers—Erie Company Records, Manuscript Collections, WRHS

Sheperd, Claude L., *Connecticut Land Company and Accompanying Records*, WRHS Tract No. 96, October, 1916

Sherman, Christopher Elias, "Original Ohio Land Subdivision . . . final report," *Ohio Cooperative Topographical Survey, Vol. 3*, Columbus, 1916 - 1933

Tappan, Abraham, *History of the Surveys West of the Cuyahoga River*, Manuscript Collections, WRHS

―――― *Sketch of the Surveys West of the Cuyahoga, 1806 - 1807*, Manuscript Collections, WRHS

HIGHWAYS AND TRAVEL

Blackman, Emily C., *History of Susquehanna County, Pennsylvania*, Philadelphia, 1873

Bronson, C. C., *The Girdled Road*, WRHS Tract No. 49, 1879

Edson, Obed, and Merrill, Georgia Drew, *History of Chautauqua County, New York*, Boston, 1894

Fitch, Winchester, *Historical Notes of Unionville, Ohio* (Harpersfield Township), Vero Beach, Fla., 1912

Griffiths, D., Jr., *Two Years Residence in the New Settlements of Ohio, with Directions to Emigrants*, London, 1835

Holditch, Robert, *The Emigrant Guide to the United States of America*, London, 1816

Hulbert, Arthur Butler, *Historic Highways of America*, 15 vols., Cleveland, 1903 (Especially Vol. 2, "Indian Thoroughfares"; Vols. 11-12, "Pioneer Roads and Experiences of Travelers")

Hutchins, Thomas, *A Topographical Description of Virginia, Pennsylvania, Maryland and North Carolina*, Cleveland, 1904

Melish, John, *Travels in the United States of America in the years 1806, 1807, 1809, 1810, and 1811*, Belfast, 1818 (best edition)

New York State Historical Association, *History of the State of New York*, 10 vols., New York, 1933-37. (Especially Vol 5: "Conquering the Wilderness")

Riddle, A. G., *History of Geauga and Lake Counties, Ohio*, Philadelphia, 1876

Spafford, Horatio Gates, ed., *Gazetteer of the State of New York*, Albany, 1813

Tryon, Warren S., ed. and comp., *A Mirror for Americans, Life and Manners in the United States, 1790 - 1870*, 3 vols., Chicago, 1952. (Especially Chapter 28, Vol. 3, "Connecticut Canaan, 1821")

Williams, William W., *History of Ashtabula County, Ohio*, Philadelphia, 1878

Zimm, Louise Seymour, ed., *Southeastern New York, a History of the Counties of Ulster, Dutchess, Orange, Rockland and Putnam*, New York, 1946

THE OHIO CANAL

Dial, George White, "The Construction of the Ohio Canals", *Ohio Archaeological & Historical Publications*, Vol. XIII, Columbus, 1904

Finn, Chester E., "The Ohio Canals, Public Enterprises on the Frontier," *Ohio State Archaeological & Historical Quarterly*, Vol. 51, No. 1. Jan.-March, 1942

Galbreath, C. B., *Ohio Canals*, Springfield, Ohio, 1910

Kilbourn, John, ed., *Public Documents Concerning the Ohio Canals*, Columbus, 1832

McClelland, C. F., and Huntington, C. C., *History of the Ohio Canals*, Columbus, 1905

Nye, Pearl R., and Thomas, Cloea, *Scenes and Songs of the Ohio-Erie Canal*, Columbus, 1952

Porter, Burton P., *Old Canal Days*, Columbus, 1942